Gettysburg Field Guide

A comprehensive tour of the Gettysburg Battlefield

Contents

Auto Tour Map .... page 4
Visitor Center .... page 6
McPherson Ridge .... page 13
Oak Hill .... page 24
Oak Ridge .... page 28
Seminary Ridge .... page 32
North Carolina Memorial .... page 33
Virginia Memorial .... page 37
Pitzer Woods .... page 40
Warfield Ridge .... page 42
Little Round Top .... page 46
Devil's Den .... page 52
The Wheatfield .... page 58
The Peach Orchard .... page 60
Trostle Farm .... page 62
Father Corby .... page 64
Pennsylvania Memorial .... page 66
Spangler's Spring .... page 68
Culp's Hill .... page 70
High Water Mark .... page 74
Bibliography & Credits .... page 80

AUTO TOUR MAP

Map Legend

- Self-guiding Auto Tour
- Detour to additional tour stop
- One-way traffic
- Trail
- **8** National Park tour stop
- **8a** Additional tour stop
- **P** Parking
- Restrooms
- Picnic area
- *York Pike* Historic road name

Notice: The TravelBrains tour route follows the official National Park auto tour route with a few exceptions. On four occasions the tour stops have been changed to provide you with a more in-depth look at the battlefield. The altered tour stops are identified on the map with blue circles and a letter **8a**. Please consult the map prior to departing to each tour stop.

Map Labels

- Amphitheater
- **6** Pitzer Woods
- Observation Tower
- West Confederate Ave
- WARFIELD RIDGE
- **7** Warfield Ridge
- **5** Virginia Memorial
- SEMINARY
- Rose Farm
- The Peach Orchard
- **10** The Peach Orchard
- Sickles Ave
- South Confederate Avenue
- **8a** Devil's Den
- **9** The Wheatfield
- Crawford Ave
- Ayres Ave
- Wheatfield Road
- **10a** Trostle Farm
- GETTYSBURG NATIONAL MILITARY PARK
- Codori Farm
- Plum Run
- BIG ROUND TOP
- Warren Avenue
- **8** Little Round Top
- Sykes Avenue
- United States Ave
- **12** Pennsylvania Memorial
- Copse of Trees
- The Angle
- **15** High Water Mark
- Wright Avenue
- Hancock Ave
- Sedgwick Ave
- **10b** Father Corby
- Pleasonton Ave
- Meade's Headquarters
- CEMETERY RIDGE
- Taneytown Road
- 134
- Granite School House Lane
- Visitor Center / Begin Auto Tour / Guides
- Hunt Ave
- Baltimore Pike
- **13** Spangler's Spring

Civil War Timeline

- Abraham Lincoln Inaugurated • Mar 4
- Manassas, VA • July 21
- Wilson's Creek, MO • Aug 10
- Fort Sumter, SC • April 12-14
- Ball's Bluff, VA • Oct 21
- Pea Ridge, AR • March 7-8
- Fort Henry & Fort Donelson, TN • Feb 6-16
- Shiloh, TN • April 6-7
- Seven Day's Battle, VA • June 25-July 1
- Manassas, VA • Aug 29-30
- Antietam, MD • Sept 17
- Siege of Vicksburg, MS • May 19-July
- Chancellorsville, VA • May 1-4
- Perryville, KY • Oct 8
- Stones River, TN • Dec 31-J
- Fredericksburg, VA • Dec 13

1861 | **1862**

Auto Tour Map

Your Guide: Wayne Motts

Military historian, Wayne E. Motts, is the CEO of the National Civil War Museum. Since 1988, Wayne has been a licensed battlefield guide at Gettysburg National Military Park and has given thousands of tours of the battlefield to visitors from all over the world. Today, Wayne will guide you to the essential locations on the battlefield and share the stories of the men and women who participated in the Civil War's defining moment.

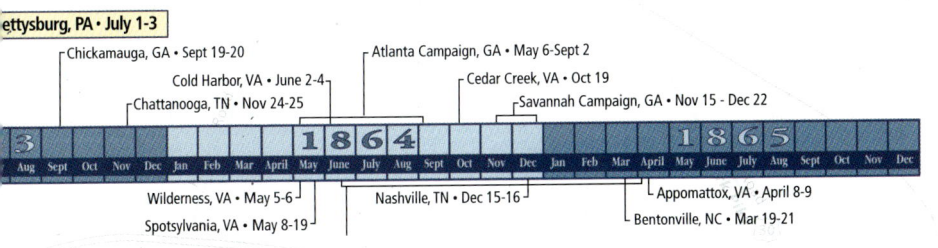

Gettysburg, PA • July 1-3
Chickamauga, GA • Sept 19-20
Cold Harbor, VA • June 2-4
Chattanooga, TN • Nov 24-25
Atlanta Campaign, GA • May 6-Sept 2
Cedar Creek, VA • Oct 19
Savannah Campaign, GA • Nov 15 - Dec 22
Wilderness, VA • May 5-6
Nashville, TN • Dec 15-16
Appomattox, VA • April 8-9
Spotsylvania, VA • May 8-19
Bentonville, NC • Mar 19-21

Visitor Center

Army of the Potomac

Total Strength:
93,000 troops
356 cannons

Meade

● I Corps — Reynolds
♣ II Corps — Hancock
♦ III Corps — Sickles
✠ V Corps — Sykes
✚ VI Corps — Sedgwick
) XI Corps — Howard
★ XII Corps — Slocum
Cavalry Corps — Pleasonton

Army of Northern Virginia

Total Strength:
75,000 troops
275 cannons

Lee

I Corps — Longstreet
II Corps — Ewell
III Corps — Hill
Cavalry — Stuart

Union troops wore distinctive symbols (left) to indicate which corps they belonged to.

Confederate corps were typically named after their commanders.

Military Hierarchy

These symbols are used on the maps in this book to denote the general locations of troops.

⊠ xxxx	Army
⊠ xxx	Corps
⊠ xx	Division
⊠ x	Brigade
⊠ |||	Regiment

Military Symbols

Infantry ⊠   Cavalry ◢   Artillery ●

Battlefield Casualties of the Civil War

Gettysburg was the bloodiest battle of the Civil War. After three days of fighting, over 51,000 soldiers were killed, wounded, or missing.

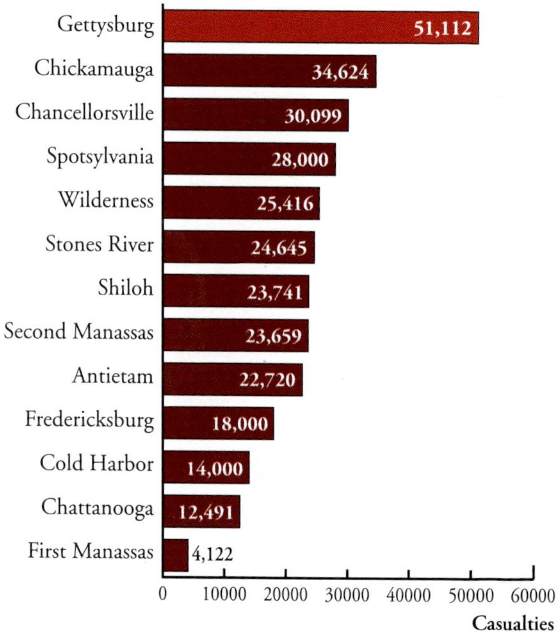

Battle	Casualties
Gettysburg	51,112
Chickamauga	34,624
Chancellorsville	30,099
Spotsylvania	28,000
Wilderness	25,416
Stones River	24,645
Shiloh	23,741
Second Manassas	23,659
Antietam	22,720
Fredericksburg	18,000
Cold Harbor	14,000
Chattanooga	12,491
First Manassas	4,122

Casualties

Visitor Center

Abraham Lincoln

Four and a half months after the Battle of Gettysburg, President Lincoln traveled to Gettysburg to dedicate a portion of the battlefield as a national cemetery. His brief speech became one of the most important speeches in American history – the Gettysburg Address.

Four score and seven years ago, our fathers brought forth upon this continent a new nation, conceived in liberty, and dedicated to the proposition that all men are created equal.

Now we are engaged in a great civil war, testing whether that nation, or any nation so conceived and so dedicated can long endure. We are met on a great battlefield of that war. We have come to dedicate a portion of that field as a final resting place for those who here gave their lives that this nation might live. It is altogether fitting and proper that we should do this.

But, in a larger sense, we cannot dedicate - we cannot consecrate - we cannot hallow this ground. The brave men, living and dead, who struggled here have consecrated it, far above our poor power to add or detract. The world will little note, nor long remember, what we say here, but it can never forget what they did here. It is for us the living, rather, to be dedicated here to the unfinished work which they who fought here have thus far so nobly advanced. It is rather for us to be here dedicated to the great task remaining before us - that from these honored dead we take increased devotion to that cause for which they gave the last full measure of devotion - that we here highly resolve that these dead shall not have died in vain - that this nation, under God, shall have a new birth of freedom - and that government of the people, by the people, for the people, shall not perish from this earth.

Visitor Center

The Gettysburg Campaign

June 3 - July 3, 1863

After the Confederate victory at Chancellorsville, VA in May 1863, General Robert E. Lee decided that the time was right for an invasion north of the Mason-Dixon. Lee hoped an invasion of the North would transfer the scene of hostilities out of Virginia's farmlands and relieve pressure on the Confederate army out west in Mississippi. Even more audacious, Lee hoped that a decisive victory on Northern soil might even possibly end the Civil War.

Visitor Center

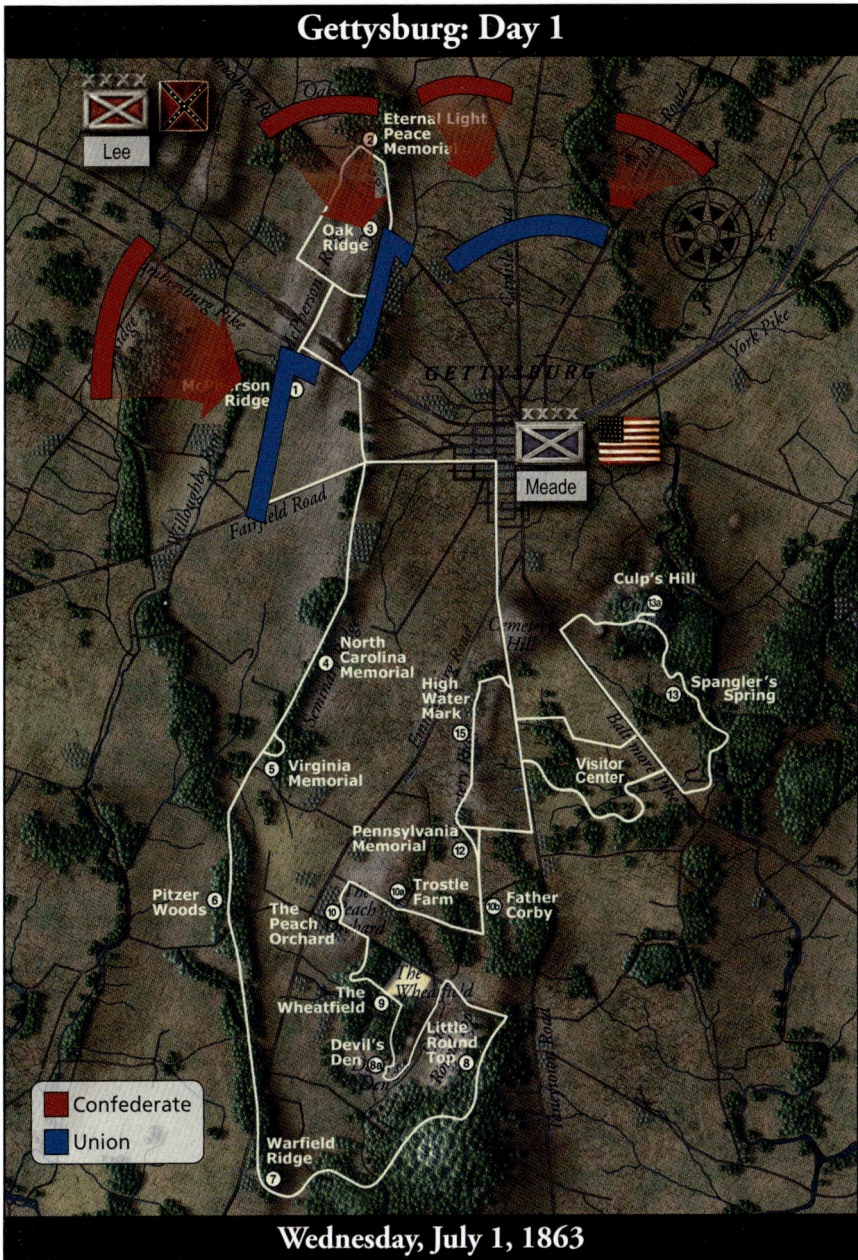

Gettysburg: Day 1

Wednesday, July 1, 1863

The fighting started early on July 1, 1863, as Union cavalry attempted to hold off the Confederate advance west of town. At around 10:30 a.m. the Union 1st Corps arrived and relieved Brigadier General John Buford's cavalrymen. By the afternoon, however, the Confederates were attacking west and north of town. The Union 1st and 11th Corps were forced to retreat through town and up to the high ground known as Cemetery Hill, south of Gettysburg.

9

Visitor Center

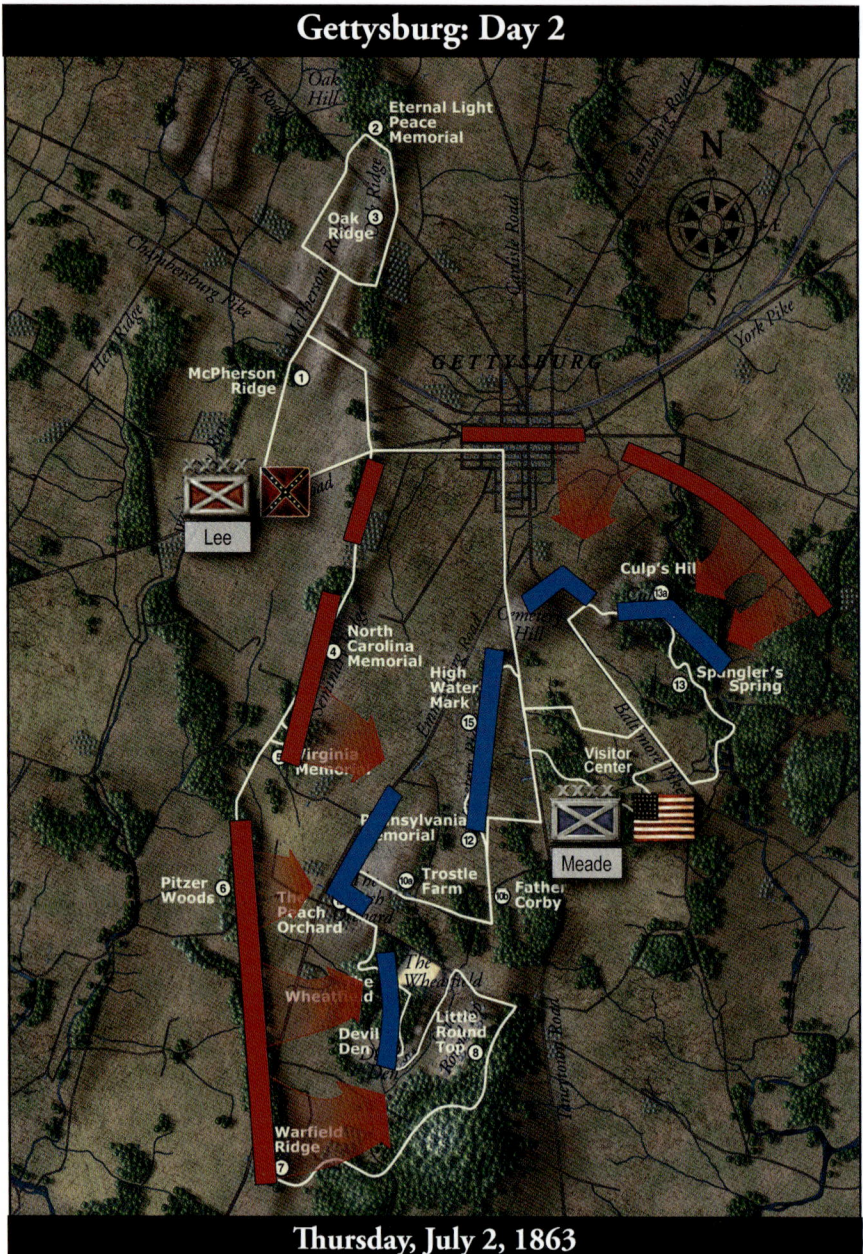

The second day of battle saw fighting on both ends of the Union line. Confederate General James Longstreet led the main thrust of the attacks on the left end of the Union Army, attacking in the areas around Little Round Top, Devil's Den, the Wheatfield, and the Peach Orchard. As the fighting concluded on the left, the hostilities continued on the far right of the Union line with Confederate assaults on Culp's Hill and East Cemetery Hill.

Visitor Center

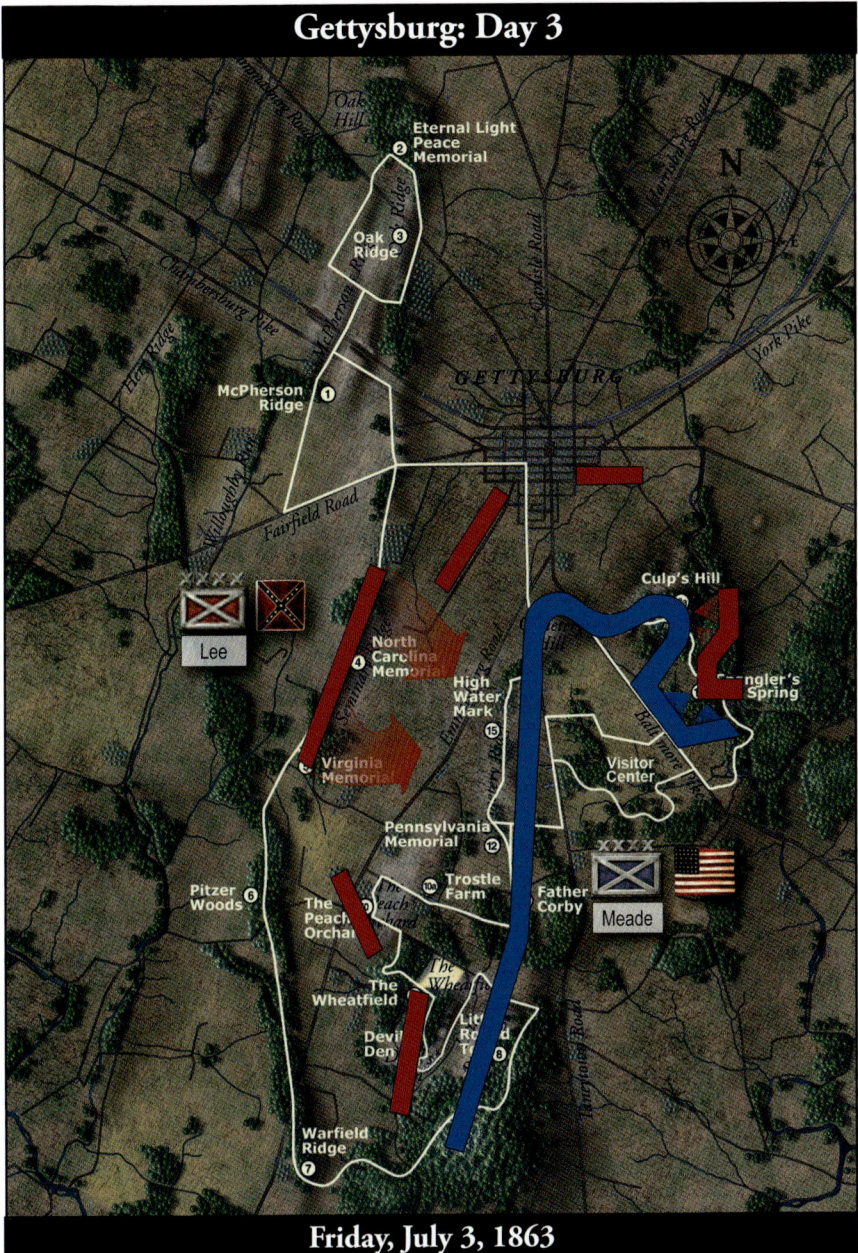

Gettysburg: Day 3

Friday, July 3, 1863

The third and final day of the conflict started early when the Federals launched attacks at the base of Culp's Hill, attempting to retake earthworks they had lost the evening before. The fighting lasted nearly seven hours. By late morning, the Union Army had retaken their trenches and the Confederates on that end of the battlefield were spent. Following a brief lull, Lee launched his final attack, Pickett's Charge. The Virginians led the way, as the Confederates attempted and failed to crush the center of the Union line.

Visitor Center

Battlefield Markers

Confederate Brigade Markers

Brigade markers with round bases identify Confederate brigades. The inscription on the plate describes the position and action of the brigade during the battle. Confederate brigades were typically composed of four to six regiments with a total of approximately 1,600 men.

Union Brigade Markers

Brigade markers with square bases identify Union brigades. The inscription on the plate describes the position and action of the brigade during the battle. Union brigades were typically composed of four to six regiments with a total of approximately 1,500 men.

Flank Markers

These small stone markers are used to identify the general location of the right and left flanks, or ends of regiments.

Battery Tablets

These plaques describe the action of artillery batteries during the conflict. Union batteries usually contained six guns; Confederate batteries, four.

Headquarters Markers

Cannon tubes that point skyward mark the approximate location of Union and Confederate headquarters during the battle. They were placed on the battlefield to identify where General Lee, General Meade and their corps commanders had headquarters.

Corps & Division Markers

These large markers indicate the general location of army corps and divisions of both armies. The plaques on the front of the markers identify the commander of the unit and describe the action in which they participated.

McPherson Ridge

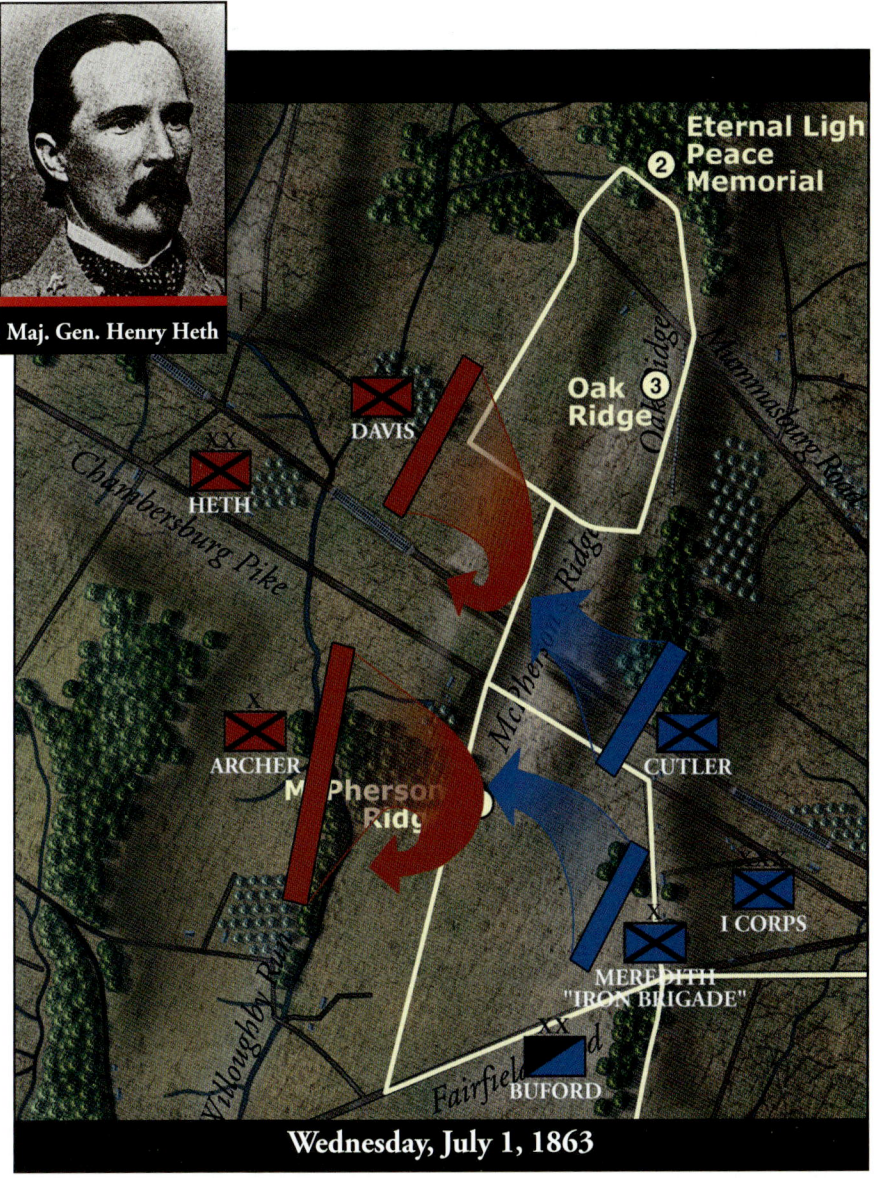

Wednesday, July 1, 1863

At approximately 10:30 a.m. on the morning of July 1, the lead elements of the Union 1st Corps arrived on the battlefield and relieved the cavalrymen of General Buford's Division. After an intense fight, the Federals were able to turn back the Confederate attack, for the moment.

Note: Battlefield maps in this guide book reflect roads and tree lines that were present at the time of the battle. The modern day auto tour route has been superimposed onto the historic terrain.

McPherson Ridge

When Union General John Buford reached the town of Gettysburg on June 30, he received reports of Confederate activity in the area. Buford was convinced that a major confrontation was imminent and recognized the importance of the high ground south of Gettysburg. Ordering his soldiers to dismount, Buford instructed them to

McPherson Ridge

defend the ridgelines west of town until the infantry could arrive. Buford knew what was at stake, and that his force of 2,900 men would soon feel the weight of a superior Confederate enemy marching at that moment toward Gettysburg. Speaking to one of his officers, Buford said, *"They will attack you in the morning and they will come booming - skirmishers three deep. You will have to fight like the devil until supports arrive."*

Brigadier General John Buford is pictured seated with members of his staff.

McPherson Ridge

The Iron Brigade

The famed "Iron Brigade" was composed of five regiments from the Midwest: the 2nd, 6th and 7th Wisconsin, the 19th Indiana, and the 24th Michigan.

The brigade earned their nickname following the hard fighting they did at the Battle of South Mountain in Maryland. Depicted above, in the painting by Dale Gallon, is Colonel Henry Morrow rallying his men of the 24th Michigan as the Iron Brigade fell back towards the Lutheran Theological Seminary on July 1, 1863.

McPherson Ridge

Men of Iron by Dale Gallon
Courtesy of Gallon Historical Art, Gettysburg, PA

The men of the Iron Brigade were also known as "The Black Hat Boys" because of the black regular army Hardee hats they wore. The horn insignia on the Hardee hat (right) represents the infantry branch of the army.

17

McPherson Ridge

Brig. General James Archer | **Maj. General Abner Doubleday**

During the first day's fighting, Confederate General James J. Archer was captured and taken behind Union lines. Union General Abner Doubleday recognized Archer from their days in the regular army before the war and said, *"Good morning Archer! How are you? I am glad to see you."* To which Archer replied, *"Well, I am not glad to see you by a damn sight!"*

Lutheran Theological Seminary

MCPHERSON RIDGE

Maj. Gen. Reynolds

While urging the Iron Brigade into battle, Union General, John Reynolds was struck by a bullet entering the back of his head behind his right ear. He was dead before he hit the ground. Reynolds was the highest ranking Union officer to be killed at Gettysburg. The monument (left) marks the location of his death.

The famous Civil War photographer, Mathew Brady, stands in the foreground (right), as his assistant points to the location where Reynolds was shot in McPherson Woods.

McPherson Ridge

Gettysburg resident, John Burns photographed in 1863

McPherson Ridge

The Railroad Cut

Just north of the Chambersburg Pike is the famous "railroad cut." During the battle, the unfinished railroad bed that cut through McPherson's Ridge was the site of a fierce exchange of gunfire. Union troops charged the cut and captured hundreds of Confederates exposed in the ravine. The above sketch by Civil War artist Alfred Waud depicts the capture of Confederate troops in the cut.

Gettysburg Civilians

The threat of the Confederate army's invasion of the North forced Gettysburg families to grapple with a difficult decision: Do they stay and protect their property from the enemy invaders, or do they leave and protect their lives?

Almost seventy years old at the time of the battle, John Burns decided to stay. A veteran of the War of 1812, he grabbed his flintlock musket when the battle began on July 1 and headed out to see what he could do. Joining up with the Iron Brigade, Burns fought bravely, but was wounded during the fight. Following the battle, the local hero returned home to recuperate. Burns died in 1872 and was buried in Gettysburg's Evergreen Cemetery.

Mary Virginia "Jennie" Wade was staying at the home of her sister, Georgia, when the battle began. From their Baltimore Street home they could see Union troops forming on Cemetery Hill. As the soldiers filed past, Jennie offered them what water and bread she had. For the next two days, Jennie baked bread and retrieved water from the well, despite being caught between Union and Confederate sharpshooters. On July 3, around 8:00 p.m., Jennie started her last loaf of bread. As she kneaded the dough, a sharpshooter's bullet passed through two doors, striking her in the back. Jennie Wade was the only civilian killed during the battle of Gettysburg.

Statue of Jennie Wade

McPherson Ridge

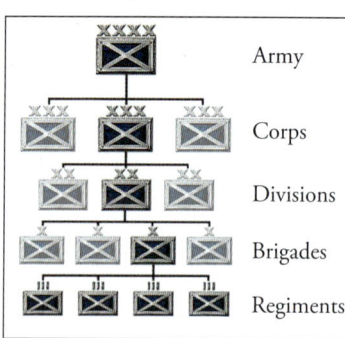

The Regiment

Regiments were the most important tactical fighting unit of the Civil War. According to regulations, a volunteer infantry regiment was supposed to consist of 1,000 men organized into ten companies of 100 men each. In reality, however, the average regimental strength was substantially less. By 1863, the average Union regiment mustered between 300-400 men.

Regimental Battle Formation

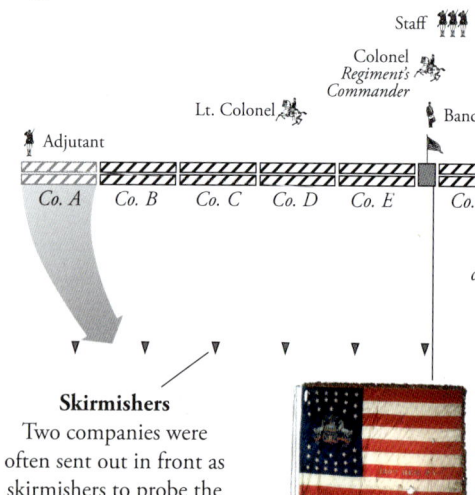

Two Ranks Deep
In combat, regiments deployed in long straight lines, two rows (ranks) deep.

Note: there was no J company. It looked to much like the letter I.

The Colors
Regiments carried their flags or "colors" in the center of the battle line. They helped guide the regiment when the din of battle made verbal commands difficult to hear. Union regiments carried two flags, Confederates one.

Skirmishers
Two companies were often sent out in front as skirmishers to probe the enemy's lines.

Smoothbore musket effective range: 100 yds.

Changing Technology

The American Civil War marked the first time in the history of warfare that rifled muskets were used in such large numbers. This weapon nearly quadrupled the effective killing range of an infantryman to nearly 400 yards under ideal circumstances. The rifle-musket achieved this astounding accuracy by etching grooves on the inside of the gun barrel. When the gun was fired, the grooves caused the bullet to spiral in flight, giving it more stability, range and accuracy.

50 yds.

McPherson Ridge

Civil War Tactics

At the time, the French military was considered to be on the leading edge of strategic and tactical theory. French tactics relied heavily on offensive force by large masses of troops. Flanking movements and frontal assaults were the primary tactics of choice.

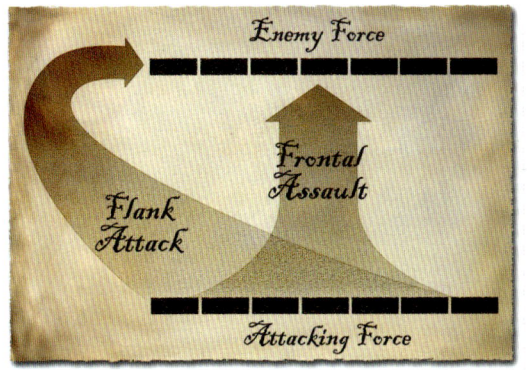

Flanking movements relied on speed and maneuverability to achieve results. Passing around the end of an enemy line, the attacker would bring his troops to bear on the opponent's flank, or end. One of the advantages to flanking the enemy was the ability to fire into the sides of the enemy line. This type of fire, also known as *enfilade*, was very effective.

The frontal assault held the allure of a quick and decisive victory. Using this tactic, troops were massed and sent head long at the enemy. Massing large numbers of men ensured that enough of the troops would arrive at the focal point of the attack to overwhelm the enemy and drive them from the field.

Many of the generals who faced each other during the Civil War witnessed this tactic achieve great success during the Mexican War, just fifteen years prior. That experience would have a lasting impact on these officers. Even though advances in firearms and cannon technology had given the advantage to the defender, many generals would continue to employ the frontal assault during the Civil War.

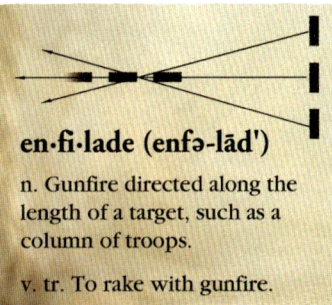

en·fi·lade (enfə-lād')
n. Gunfire directed along the length of a target, such as a column of troops.
v. tr. To rake with gunfire.

Rifle musket effective range: 300 - 400 yards

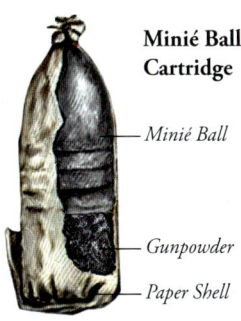

Minié Ball

(actual size)

The Minié Ball was named after French army officer Claude-Etienne Minié. Upon firing, the base of the bullet would expand in the barrel, forcing it against the rifle grooves that lined the barrel. The grooves, in turn, caused the bullet to spin, which greatly improved its accuracy.

Minié Ball Cartridge

– Minié Ball
– Gunpowder
– Paper Shell

100 yds.   150 yds.   200 yds.

23

Oak Hill

Eternal Light Peace Memorial

Dedicated in 1938, the Eternal Light Peace Memorial stands atop Oak Hill as a reminder of reconciliation between the men of the blue and gray. The idea for the monument, proposed by Union and Confederate veterans, actually began during the 50th Gettysburg reunion in 1913. Despite the financial difficulties of the Great Depression, funding for the project was eventually secured and the memorial was ready to dedicate at the 75th anniversary of the battle (above).

The keynote speaker for the event was President Franklin D. Roosevelt who spoke to crowds estimated at over 200,000. He used the opportunity to invoke some of President Abraham Lincoln's thoughts and ideas from his dedication of the Soldier's National Cemetery, the Gettysburg Address. A veteran from the Union and Confederate army each pulled one of the cords that removed the flag draped over the monument. The darker base portion is made of Maine granite while the shaft supporting the eternal flame is of Alabama limestone. Except for a brief period when the monument was electrified, the eternal flame burns continuously twenty-four hours a day.

Former enemies shake hands at the 50th anniversary of the battle

OAK HILL

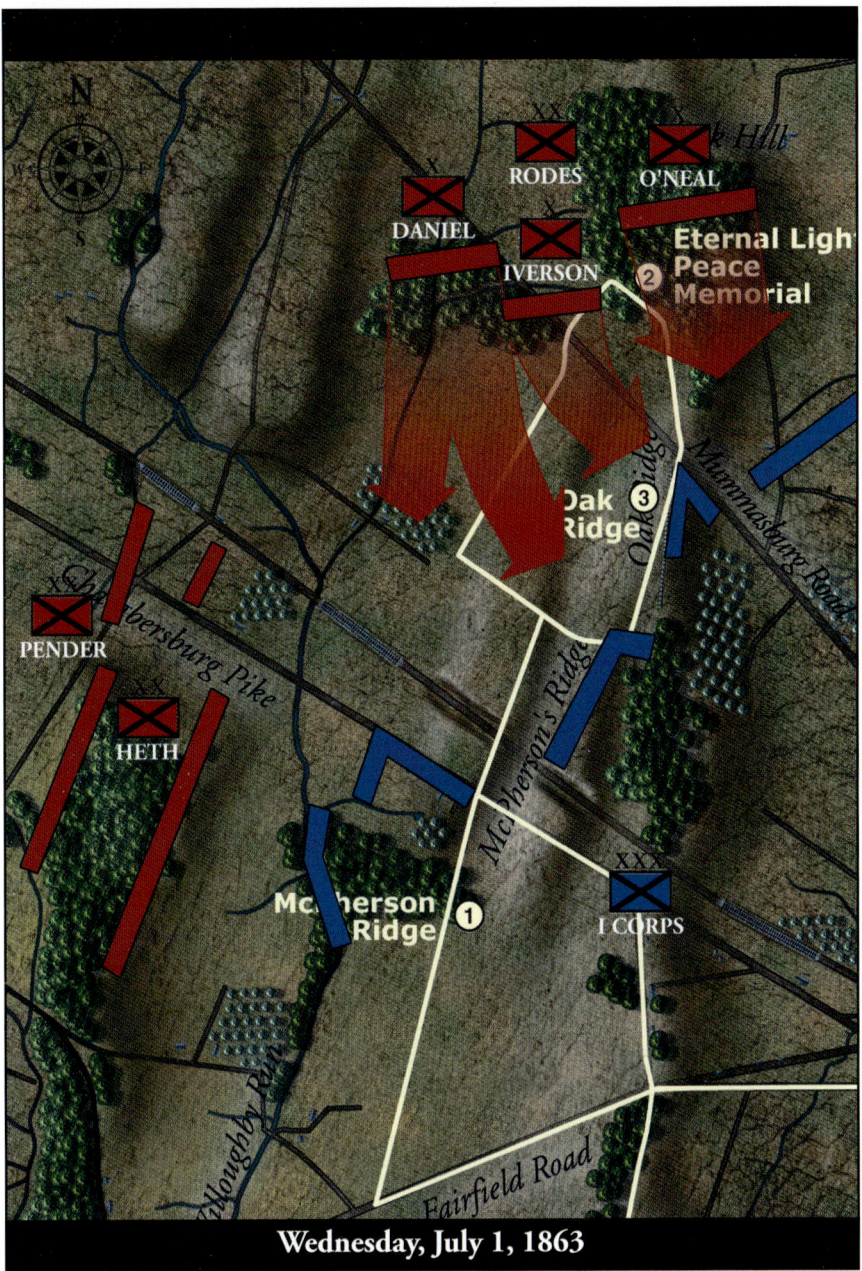

When fighting resumed on the afternoon of July 1, 1863, Confederate General Robert Rodes ordered three of his brigades to attack the right end of the Union 1st Corps. These initial assaults ended in disaster for the Confederates.

Oak Hill

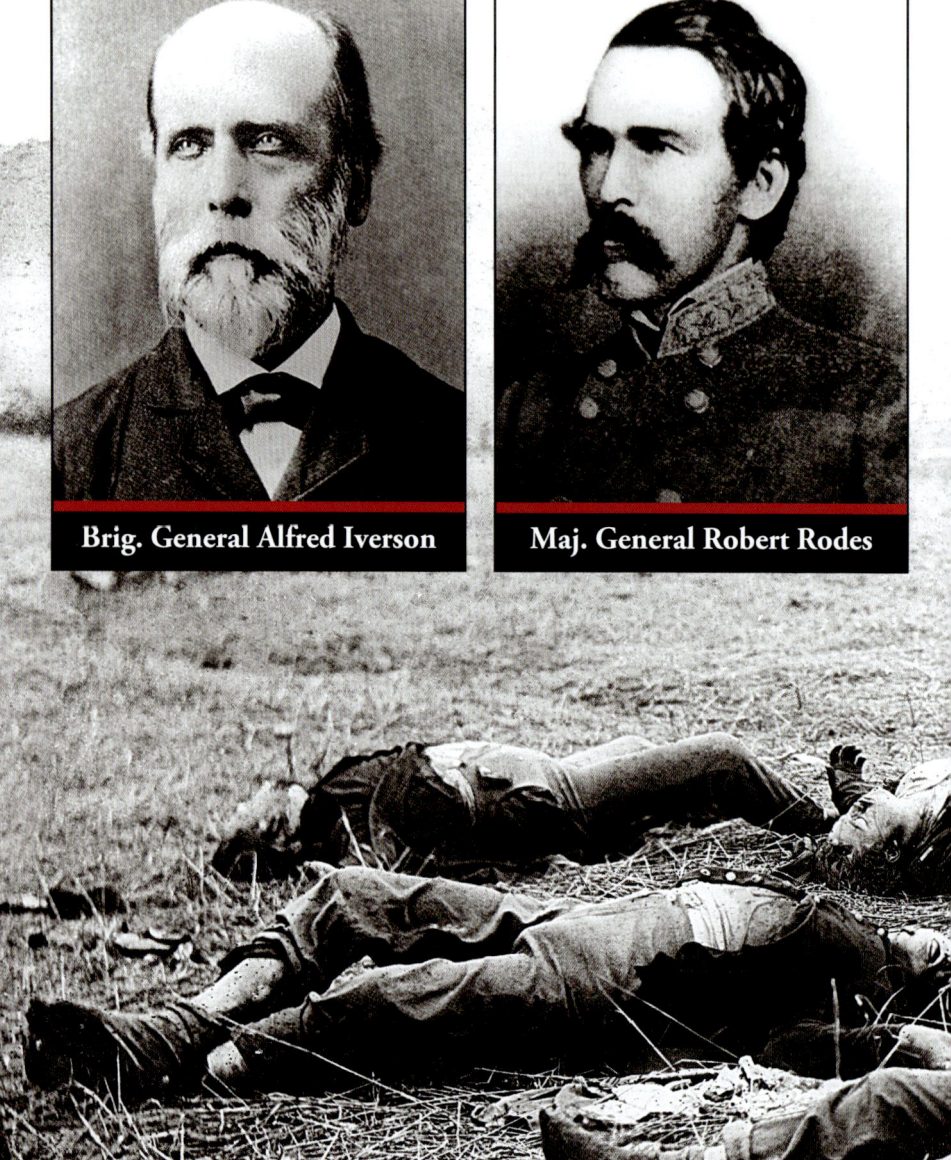

Brig. General Alfred Iverson

Maj. General Robert Rodes

Oak Hill

Oak Hill

At around 2:30 p.m. in the afternoon of July 1, Confederate infantry emerged from the woods on Oak Hill. Looking out across the Mummasburg Road, they saw what appeared to be the right end of the Union 1st Corps. General Rodes, commanding the Confederate troops on Oak Hill, believed the Union line was a threat to his own command, and resolved to hit the Yankees first. He issued orders to attack with three infantry brigades. The center brigade was a group of some 1,300 North Carolinians under the command of Brigadier General Alfred Iverson, the son of a former United States Senator.

Forming a battle line near the Mummasburg Road, Iverson's men marched in perfect formation toward the Union position along Oak Ridge. Things started to go wrong almost immediately, however. Iverson had chosen not to lead his troops in person and could, therefore, do nothing but watch as his men began drifting left toward a stone wall. Hidden behind this stone wall, on the slopes of Oak Ridge, were men of the Union 1st Corps. When Iverson's men were within close range, these Union troops sprang to their feet and let loose an absolutely terrifying volley of musketry. Over 500 North Carolinians were mowed down in an instant. They fell dead or wounded in a straight line as if on dress parade.

From General Iverson's vantage point, however, his troops appeared to be able-bodied men lying on the ground in battle formation. So when he looked out and saw white handkerchiefs being waved on the battlefield he was shocked. General Iverson believed that his men were surrendering en masse to the enemy. It was not until later that he learned that most of the men he saw were either dead or badly wounded. The men waiving the white flags were the few remaining survivors who hoped to avoid being completely annihilated. In total, nearly 900 of Iverson's North Carolinians were killed, wounded, or captured by the end of the fighting.

Originally believed to be Union casualties from the first day of fighting, later investigations revealed that they are more likely dead Union III Corps soldiers from the second day of fighting. Notice how they have no shoes. Soldiers from both sides, in desperate need of supplies, often took them from fallen comrades.

Oak Ridge

Brig. General Francis Barlow

Afternoon of July 1, 1863

The extreme right end of the Union 11th Corps was anchored across the valley on a small knoll. Today known as Barlow's Knoll, this rise of ground was named after Brigadier General Francis Barlow who attempted to defend it during the battle. What Barlow found out though, was that the knoll was particularly vulnerable to attack from several directions. At 3:30 p.m. on July 1, approximately 1,400 Georgians came screaming over fences splashing through a creek and slammed into the Union position atop the hill. These shock tactics stunned the Union soldiers and before any semblance of order could be reestablished two more Confederate brigades came crashing in from the side. The position was untenable and soon collapsed under the pressure. With the right end of the 11th Corps line unhinged, the entire Union defense began to crumble.

During the course of fighting that afternoon, the McClean house and barn was the site of one of the biggest ironies of the battle. Elements of the 45th New York infantry regiment from Syracuse, NY were ordered to the barn and surrounding areas to flush out Confederate sharpshooters. One of the soldiers present with this Union regiment was a corporal by the name of Rudolf Schwarz, a German immigrant. As Schwarz was heading to the barn, he spied Confederate prisoners being taken to the rear. One of the men he caught sight of was his own brother, dressed in a Confederate uniform and fighting with the Southern troops near Oak Hill. Immediately the two men embraced. Then parting from one another, the Confederate brother was escorted to the rear. Later that afternoon, Rudolph Schwartz, the Union soldier, was killed in action.

At the same time that the right end of the Union 11th Corps was being overrun, the Confederates launched a series of attacks up here along Oak Ridge and along McPherson's Ridge. The attacks came fast and furious and the Union 1st Corps was on the verge of collapsing. Observing this situation was

90th Pennsylvania Memorial

Eternal Light Peace Memorial

Oak Hill

McClean House and Barn

Oak Ridge

Brig. General John Robinson

Colonel Charles Tilden

Union General James Robinson in command of a division along Oak Ridge. With precious few minutes to spare, he rode over to the men of the 16th Maine, commanded by Colonel Charles Tilden. Pointing to a spot very near to where you are currently parked, Robinson ordered Tilden to, "Take that position – and hold it at any cost."

Tilden and the 298 men of the 16th Maine charged into the eye of the storm. They fought with sheer determination trying to hold off the Confederate onslaught and give the rest of the 1st Corps a chance to retire. Within a short time, they were surrounded. Colonel Tilden, recognizing that they would soon be killed or captured, resolved to deny his enemy the spoils of their victory. Grabbing his sword, he plunged the blade into the earth and broke it off at the hilt. Banding together, the remaining men of the regiment broke the staff of the regimental flag in half, tore the banner into shreds, and distributed the pieces among the survivors. Eventually 164 of the men were captured. When the men were sent off to Confederate prisons, parts of the 16th Maine flag went with them: to Libby and Belle Isle prisons near Richmond, and later, to Andersonville in Georgia. Following the American Civil War, several pieces of the flag returned once again to Gettysburg and the hallowed ground the regiment had defended to the last.

Barlow's Knoll

OAK RIDGE

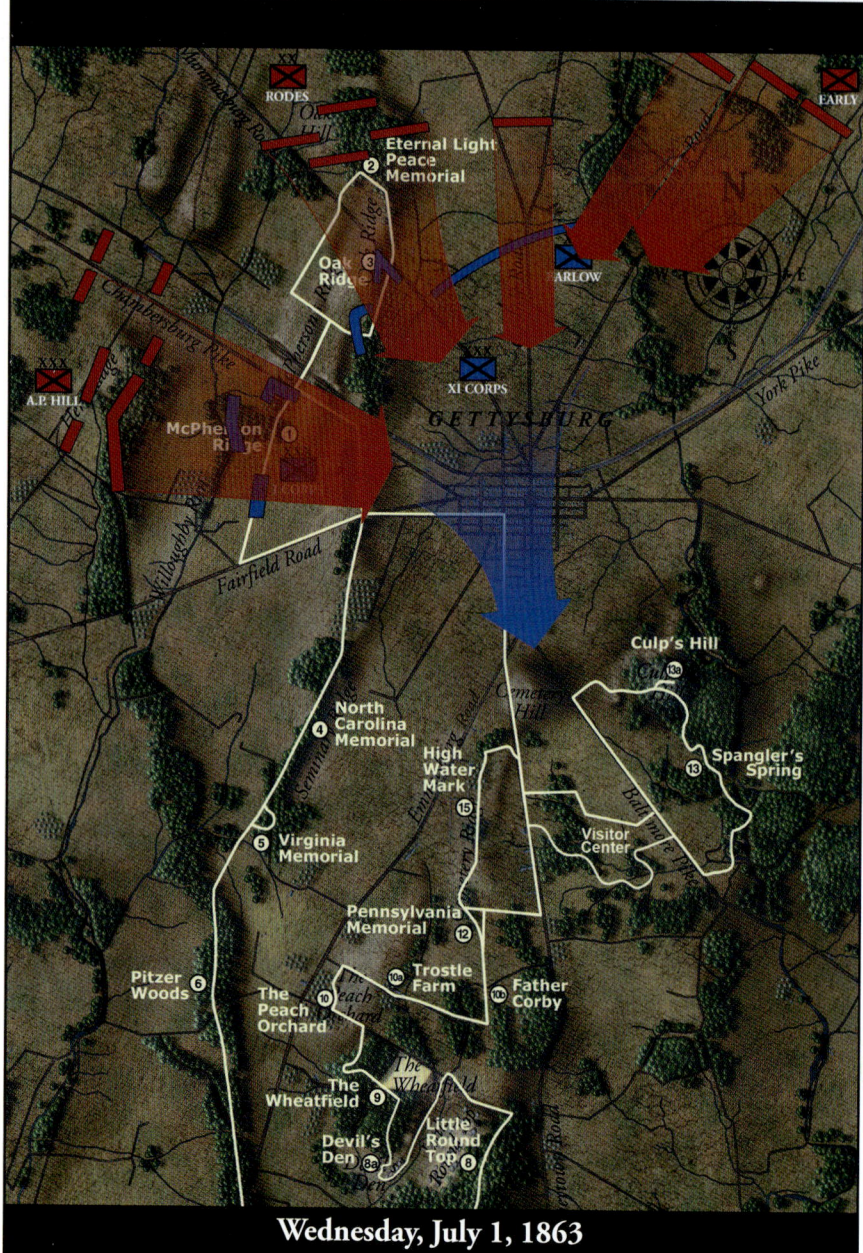

Wednesday, July 1, 1863

During the afternoon, the Union 11th Corps arrived and took up positions north of town. Soon the Confederates were attacking on all fronts west and north of Gettysburg. The pressure was too great and the Federals began to withdraw. Thousands of Union soldiers were taken prisoner trying to make their way through town and onto Cemetery Hill.

OAK RIDGE

Memorial to the 90th Pennsylvania

According to oral tradition, during the fighting here on July 1, an artillery shell smashed into a large oak tree, causing it to rain branches and pieces of splintered trunk down onto the soldiers below. A soldier with the 90th Pennsylvania Infantry spotted a nest filled with baby robins that had survived their fall to Earth. In the heat of battle the soldier picked up the nest and placed it back up in the shattered tree. The sculpture of the mother robin sitting over her babies represents the regeneration of life and the dawn of a new era of tranquility and kindness.

Gettysburg in 1863

By 1863 the town of Gettysburg numbered 2,400 inhabitants and a variety of businesses, such as tanneries, hotels, dry goods stores and carriage makers. Gettysburg also boasted two institutions of higher learning: the Lutheran Theological Seminary and Pennsylvania College (later named Gettysburg College). Both of these academic institutions would soon bear witness to operations, amputations and many a soldier's last moments on Earth.

Though it is rumored that the Confederate army arrived in Gettysburg looking for shoes, there was no shoe factory here - only local cobblers plying their trade. It was instead the road system that brought war to Gettysburg. Roughly ten roads radiated from the town, four of which converged on the center of town, also known as "The Diamond" or "Square." The northern and eastern roads led to Carlisle, Harrisburg, and York, Pennsylvania, while the southerly routes accessed Baltimore, Westminister, and Hagerstown, Maryland. These converging roads allowed Lee to gather his dispersed army as the Union Army approached.

This photograph, taken from Seminary Ridge looking east, shows the Chambersburg Pike heading towards the center of town. In the distance you can see Culp's Hill and Cemetery Hill, where the Union Army regrouped at the end of the first day of fighting.

31

Seminary Ridge

Lutheran Theological Seminary

The Lutheran Theological Seminary and neighboring Gettysburg College were founded by Samuel Simon Schmucker, a leading churchman in American Lutheran circles during the mid-19th century. An articulate Lutheran anti-slavery activist, Schmucker supported the Underground Railroad by harboring fugitive slaves in his barn.

When the Battle of Gettysburg began, most of the students and professors at the seminary evacuated the area. On the morning of July 1, General Buford utilized the cupola of the building as a vantage point for directing his troops. As the day progressed, more soldiers filed past on their way to halt the advancing Confederates. By 4:00 p.m. the Union Army could no longer hold their positions and retreated, passing through the seminary and continuing south to Cemetery Hill on the other side of town.

The building, now situated behind Confederate lines, was used as a hospital for the wounded from both armies. It would remain in use as a hospital until September when students returned to finish their studies. Today the building is known as Schmucker Hall (pictured below).

Today, Schmucker Hall is a museum. Stop in and explore the exhibits, hear the voices of duty and devotion, and stand where General Buford observed approaching Confederate forces.

The seminary's cupola became an iconic symbol of the first day's fighting at Gettysburg.

NORTH CAROLINA MEMORIAL

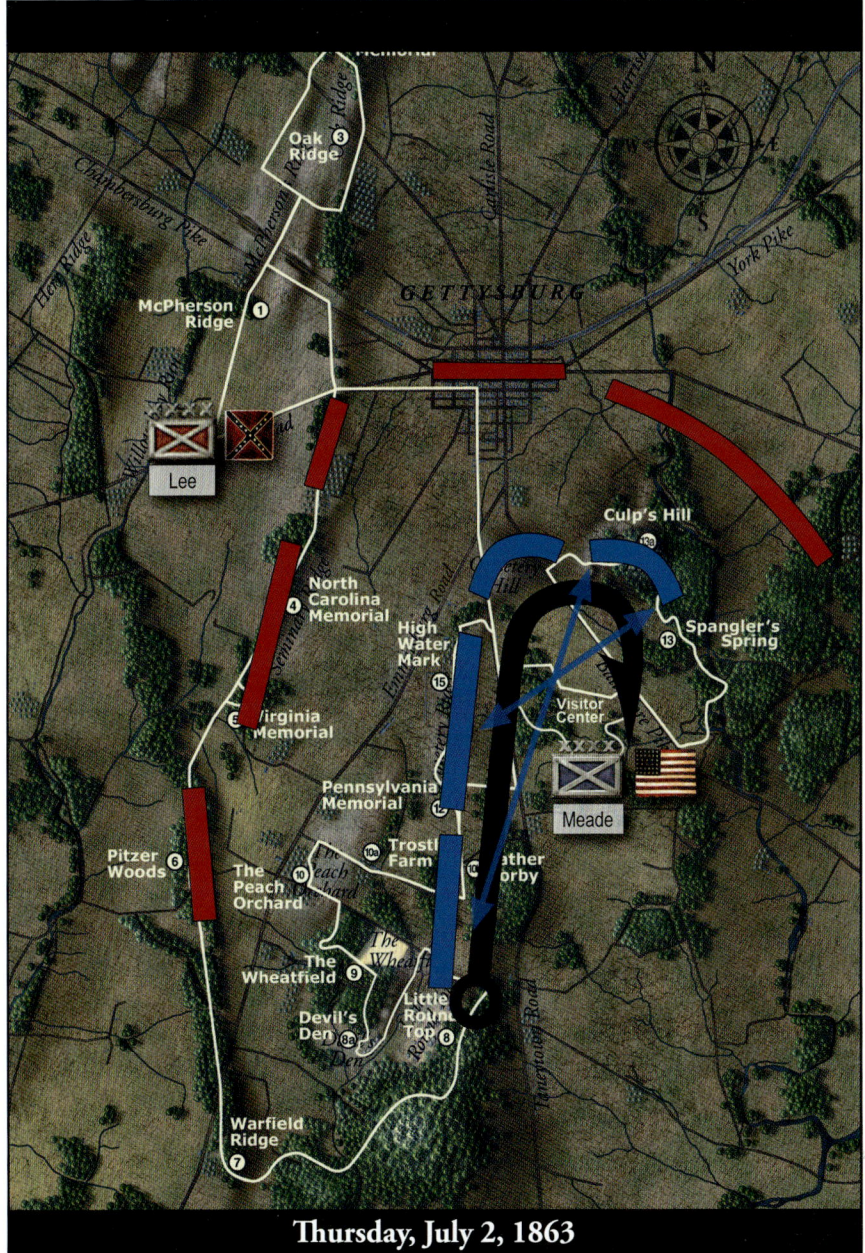

Thursday, July 2, 1863

By the afternoon of July 2, 1863, all of General George Meade's seven infantry corps had arrived and taken up positions on the hills and ridges south of town. As each Union Corps took up its respective position, the Federal line took on the shape of a fishhook. This shape allowed Meade to take advantage of interior lines to move his troops.

33

North Carolina Memorial

Artillery of the Civil War

Solid Shot

Solid shot was a round ball or elongated projectile made of solid iron. It was typically used at longer ranges against massed troops, fortifications, and enemy batteries. Solid shot (or bolts as they were called when fired from rifled cannon) were not designed to explode.

Shell

A shell was a cast iron projectile (round or elongated) filled with black powder. Different fuses allowed the artillerist to control when the shell would explode. An impact fuse exploded when it hit a target. A time fuse was started by the discharge of the cannon. Experienced artillerists could accurately time the fuse to explode the shell over the target.

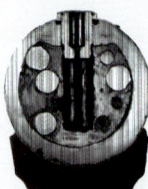

Case Shot

Case shot, sometimes called shrapnel, was a hollow iron shell (round or elongated) filled with round balls and sealed in melted rosin or sulfur. A powder charge in the core of the shell was designed to explode near the target, sending the balls and twisted fragments of iron ripping through soldiers and horses.

Canister

Canister was a tin can filled with iron balls (a little smaller than the size of golf balls) packed in sawdust. This type of ammunition effectively turned the cannon into a large shotgun. It was used at close range against infantry. In extreme cases, double and triple canister rounds were packed into the cannon and fired.

The Artillery Crew

A well-drilled crew could load and fire a cannon about three times per minute. A gun crew of ten men was ideal. A lieutenant and a sergeant gave orders; a gunner aimed the cannon; and the remaining seven crew members, each identified with a number, loaded, fired, and cleaned the cannon.

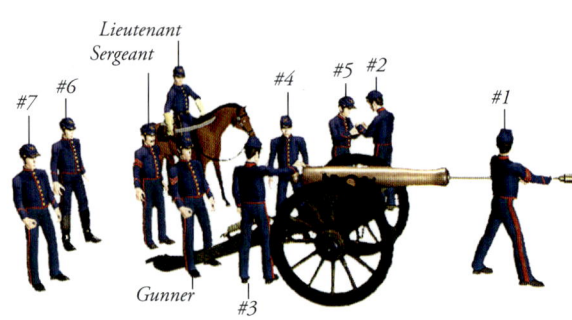

0 yds.

34

North Carolina Memorial

12-Pounder Napoleon

This famous style of cannon was named after Emperor Napoleon III of France. The term "12-Pounder" comes from the twelve-pound artillery round it fired. By the end of the Civil War it was by far the most widely used artillery piece in both armies. It had an effective range of one mile and could fire solid shot, shell, case shot, and canister rounds. Made of bronze, the tube turns green as it oxidizes over time.

10-Pounder Parrott Rifle

Made of cast iron with a wrought iron jacket, these cannon were named for its designer, Robert Parrott, of the West Point Foundry. Cast iron guns were better at maintaining the rifle grooves on the inside of the tubes (bronze was too soft), but they were brittle and could crack or explode on discharge. Parrott devised a solution to this problem by wrapping a hot band of iron around the breech, or base, of the tube.

3-Inch Ordnance Rifle

Made entirely of wrought iron, the 3-inch ordnance rifle was expensive and time consuming to produce. Its durability and accuracy, however, made it a favorite among artillerists on both sides of the war. The name of the cannon is derived from the diameter of the gun's bore.

  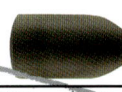

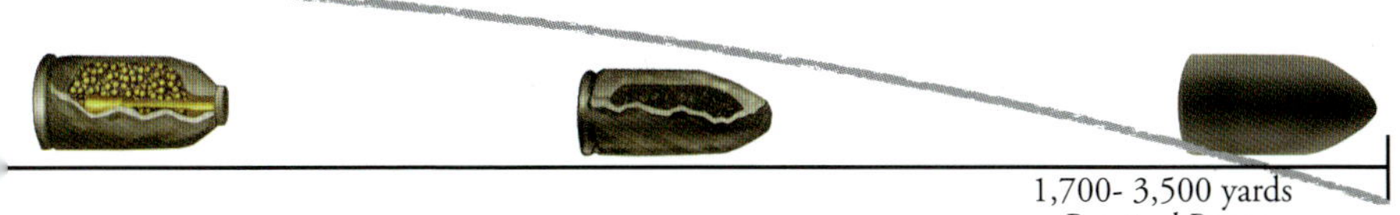

1,700- 3,500 yards
Practical Range

North Carolina Memorial

North Carolina Memorial

Dedicated in 1929, the North Carolina State Memorial was one of the earliest southern state memorials on the battlefield. The monument is located in the general location where a brigade of North Carolinians emerged from the woods heading for the center of the Union line during Pickett's Charge. It depicts a wounded officer urging his men forward as he points to the enemy. The color bearer in the statue was actually modeled after a man named Orren Randolph Smith, who is credited with designing the first Confederate National Flag, the "Stars and Bars."

The Stars and Bars

Virginia Memorial

Virginia Memorial

Dedicated on June 8, 1917, the Virginia memorial was the first Confederate state monument on the battlefield of Gettysburg. Depicted atop the memorial is General Robert E. Lee, riding his horse, Traveller.

On the final day of the battle, Lee positioned himself near this location to view the frontal assault that would become known as, "Pickett's Charge." The plan called for nearly 12,500 troops, stretched out almost a mile, to attack the center of the Union line. Lee ordered his forces to converge on a single point: "the copse of trees" — a small cluster of trees on an otherwise barren section of Cemetery Ridge that offered little cover for defending troops.

General George E. Pickett and his fresh Virginia troops had the task of leading the assault. To do so, they would have to cross nearly a mile of open fields to reach the center of the Union line. It is hard to imagine what the men of Pickett's division were thinking and feeling just before they took their first step into the terrifying spectacle that awaited them: cannon shells bursting overhead and the sound of minié balls zipping through the hot July air. If you can imagine the prospect of an almost certain death or wounding, then you can start to appreciate the kind of courage that it must have taken to stand elbow to elbow here on the battlefield on July 3, 1863.

Virginia Memorial

General Robert E. Lee

After graduating next to the top of his class at West Point in 1829, Robert E. Lee served with distinction in the United States army for thirty-two years. So revered was Robert E. Lee as a battlefield commander, that on the eve of the Civil War, President Lincoln authorized War Department officials to offer Lee command of a newly raised army to restore the Union.

When Virginia voted to secede from the Union, however, Lee was forced to make a difficult choice: stay with United States army or follow the path of his fellow Virginians. Lee followed his conscience and submitted his resignation.

Leaving his estate in Arlington, VA behind, Lee headed to Richmond, VA, where he assumed command of the Virginia state forces on April 23, 1861. Almost one year later Lee was placed in full command of the Army of Northern Virginia.

Virginia Memorial

Major General Montgomery Meigs

One of Lee's acquaintances in the regular army prior to the Civil War was a man by the name of General Montgomery Meigs. Meigs was the Chief Quartermaster of the United States Army, headquartered in Washington. Despite the fact that Meigs was born in Georgia and had a brother serving in the Confederacy, he harbored deep resentment towards former army officers who had joined the Southern cause. So deep was his hatred for Lee, and his decision to fight against the United States, that when the Federal government seized Lee's former Arlington House estate because of $92.07 worth of delinquent taxes, Meigs devised a plan to ensure Lee could never again return to his home. One way of doing that was to convert the estate into a cemetery for the Union dead. So, under the direction of General Meigs, Lee's beloved Arlington House quickly became Arlington National Cemetery. Just next to the house in the rose garden were some of the first burials of Union soldiers. In 1864, Meigs' own son was killed while serving in the Union Army, and buried on the grounds. When Meigs died in 1892, the general was laid to rest next to his son just a few feet from Lee's former home.

PITZER WOODS

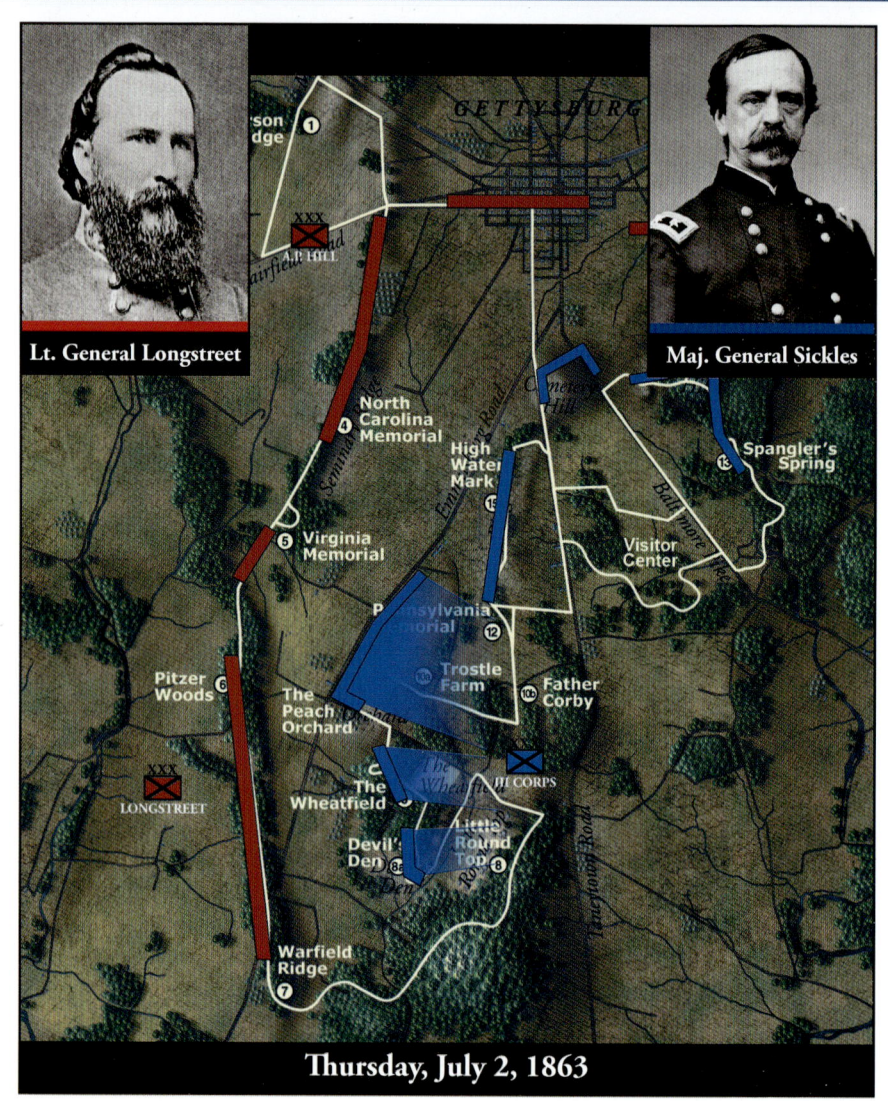

Lt. General Longstreet

Maj. General Sickles

Thursday, July 2, 1863

General Daniel E. Sickles, commander of the Union 3rd Corps had taken it upon himself, without permission from his superiors, to march his 10,000 man force out in front of the rest of the Union line to occupy what he believed to be superior ground, the elevated ridge in the Peach Orchard. Sickles' decision would have grave repercussions for the men of the 3rd Corps and would threaten the entire Union Army as the days' events unfolded. The Confederates were not the only ones surprised at Sickles' new line. General Meade, commander of the Union Army, was furious to learn that Sickles had taken it upon himself to advance his men into the Peach Orchard. He even met with Sickles to inquire why this had been done and to see if anything could be done to rectify the situation. When Sickles offered to return to his original position, Meade snapped back, *"You can not hold this position, but the enemy will not let you get away without a fight...."* It was nearly at that instant that the Confederate assault began on the Union left. The bloodiest day of Gettysburg had commenced.

Pitzer Woods

Mississippi Memorial

Dedicated in 1973, the Mississippi State Memorial was sculpted by Donald DeLue. It is located in the area where Confederate General William Barksdale's Brigade of Mississippians was positioned prior to attacking the Union troops in the Peach Orchard on July 2, 1863. The monument commemorates the bravery and sacrifice of the Mississippi soldiers who fought here at the Battle of Gettysburg. Depicted are two Mississippi infantrymen during the attack on July 2. In the fierce fighting that ensued, one Mississippi soldier has fallen mortally wounded. Grasping his musket as a club, the other soldier stops beside his comrade to defend their fallen colors.

Louisiana Memorial

Dedicated in 1971, the Louisiana State Memorial was also sculpted by Donald DeLue. It consists of a bronze statue of two figures on a polished green granite base. The reclining figure represents a fallen artilleryman. The soldier grasps a Confederate battle flag close to his chest, as the "Spirit of the Confederacy" rises over the soldier's body. Sitting in the reeds beneath the female "Spirit" figure is the dove of peace. Held aloft in her right hand is a flaming cannonball, symbolizing the artillery and ordnance arms of the army.

WARFIELD RIDGE

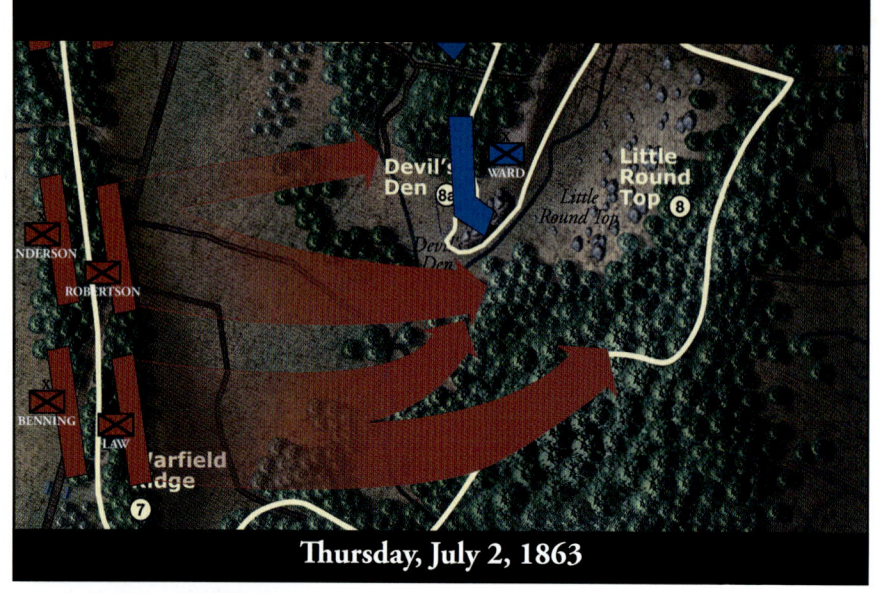

Thursday, July 2, 1863

Brig. General Evander Law

EVANDER LAW'S BRIGADE

You are now at the extreme right end of the Confederate line on the afternoon of July 2, 1863. General Evander Law's Alabamians occupied this position prior to the attack. Law's brigade is a perfect example of the hardship and physical punishment soldiers endured during the American Civil War.

At the end of the previous day's fighting, Law's men were still twenty-five miles away from Gettysburg when they received word that they were needed at the front. After a grueling twelve hour march, they were ordered into line and participated in Longstreet's march and countermarch over to this position. By the time they reached this location at 3:30 p.m., they were exhausted.

Many of the men, including those from the 15th Alabama, were dehydrated from their rapid march to the field and the scorching temperatures. While waiting for the attack to start, twenty-two men of the 15th Alabama were sent out to find water and fill canteens. Unfortunately, during their search for something to drink, all twenty-two of these Confederate soldiers were captured. The regiment, already fatigued from a hard march and now without drinking water, was about to advance headlong into some of the toughest fighting on the fields of Gettysburg. At around 4:00 p.m. on July 2, the Alabamians stepped off in the direction of a rocky hill, today known as Little Round Top, unaware that some tenacious soldiers from Maine would soon be in their front.

Warfield Ridge

Soldiers and Sailors of the Confederacy

Dedicated in 1965, the memorial was established to honor the bravery of all the men who fought in the Confederate armies and navies. After careful consideration, Gettysburg was chosen as the ideal location for the monument because it represents the "High Water Mark" of the Confederacy.

It is the third memorial at Gettysburg sculpted by Donald DeLue. The bronze statue depicts a charging Confederate color bearer calling for his fellow soldiers to push forward. Inscribed in the pink granite base are the names of the southern states that contributed soldiers to the Confederate Army. The name Walter Washington Williams is engraved on the backside of the monument. He was originally believed to be the last surviving Civil War soldier. It was later discovered to be untrue.

43

WARFIELD RIDGE

Breechloaders and Greencoats by Dale Gallon
Courtesy of Gallon Historical Art, Gettysburg, PA

As Law's men left the cover of Warfield Ridge to attack the left end of the Union line, a small but elite group of Union soldiers stood in there way. The green clad Berdan Sharpshooters were expert marksmen attached to the 2nd United States Sharpshooters Regiment. To qualify as a sharpshooter a man had to fire ten bullets into a 10-inch target at a distance of 200 yards, and no bullet could strike the target more than five inches from the bull's eye.

44

WARFIELD RIDGE

The weapon of choice for Berdan's Sharpshooters was a Sharps rifle. Pictured above is a New Model 1859 version. These breech-loading rifles were easier and quicker to reload than a rifle-musket.

LITTLE ROUND TOP

Colonel Joshua Chamberlain

Colonel Joshua Chamberlain, with the 350 men of the 20th Maine, held the extreme left of the Union line. Colonel Strong Vincent had given Chamberlain the order to hold his ground "*at all hazards.*" If the Confederates attacked and overtook the 20th Maine's position, the entire Union line would be compromised. For nearly two hours, the 20th Maine withstood several waves of Confederate assaults. Lines of men charged and fired at each other from close range. Eventually, ammunition started to run low. His men were exhausted, outnumbered, and forced to collect ammunition from the dead and dying. In a final act of desperation, Chamberlain ordered his men to fix bayonets and charge the enemy. Recalling the incident years later, he said the order, *"ran like fire along the line, from man to man, and rose into a shout, with which they sprang upon the enemy now not more than thirty yards away."* The charge worked and the 20th Maine saved the Union line. Chamberlain would later receive the Medal of Honor for this courageous act.

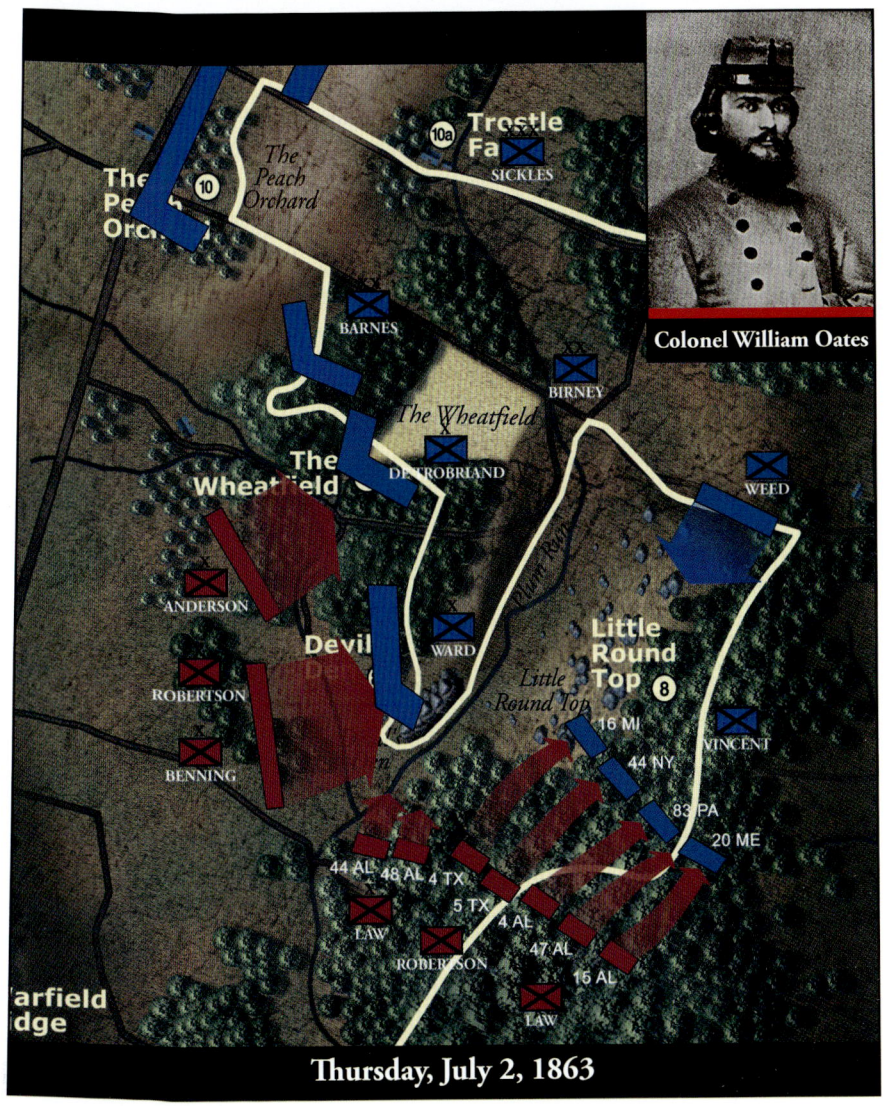

LITTLE ROUND TOP

Thursday, July 2, 1863

Colonel William Oates

Leading the 15th Alabama Infantry, Colonel William Oates attempted to flank the Union line on Little Round Top, but could not push past the stubborn defense of Chamberlain's 20th Maine.

20TH MAINE MONUMENT

Erected in 1886, the 20th Maine monument stands on a boulder near the location where the regiment's color sergeant, Andrew Tozier, appeared through the battle smoke. The names of the thirty-eight men from the regiment who gave their lives in the defense of Little Round Top are inscribed on the monument.

LITTLE ROUND TOP

General Meade's chief engineer, General Gouverneur K. Warren, realized that something was amiss on the left of the Union line on July 2, 1863. General Meade had ordered him to check on the left end of the Union line. When Warren ascended Little Round Top, he was shocked at what he saw — Expecting part

Brig. General Gouverneur Warren

The monument to Gouverneur Warren on Little Round Top depicts the general looking southwest in the direction of the Confederates.

LITTLE ROUND TOP

of General Sickles' 3rd Corps holding the hill, General Warren met only a few signalmen on its crest. Warren sent word to Meade that a division was needed to hold this critical terrain. Then turning his attention to locating the Confederate's position, Warren requested a battery in Devil's Den to fire into the trees along Warfield Ridge. *"As the shot went whistling through the air the sound of it reached the enemy's troops and caused every one to look in the direction of it. This motion revealed to me the glistening of gun-barrels and bayonets of the enemy's line of battle . . . far outflanking the position of any of our troops… The discovery was intensely thrilling…and almost appalling."*

Little Round Top

Little Round Top

In 1863, Little Round Top appeared much as it does today, cleared of trees on its western slope. This made it an ideal location for artillery. Big Round Top, to the south, is higher in elevation, but it was fully wooded and therefore not useful for such a purpose. If the Confederates captured Little Round Top and placed their artillery there, they would be in a position to fire north at the Union line all the way to Cemetery Hill. They could also capture the Taneytown Road, located directly east of the hill, an important Union supply route running south from Gettysburg.

If Little Round Top was taken by Longstreet's men, they could have effectively bottled up a large part of Meade's army, forcing them to retire down a single open road, the Baltimore Pike.

Little Round Top

Little Round Top

140th New York Infantry Monument

Colonel Patrick O'Rorke graduated at the head of his class at West Point two years before the battle of Gettysburg. On July 2, 1863, O'Rorke arrived at the summit of Little Round Top just in time to bolster the right end of the Union line as it was being overrun. Over 500 men of O'Rorke's regiment plunged down the slopes and slammed into the Confederate lines. O'Rorke was killed in the desperate fighting, but his quick action pushed the Confederates back down the hill. The monument to his regiment now stands in the approximate location where O'Rorke was killed by a bullet wound to the neck.

Plum Run

Big Round Top

Devil's Den

Devil's Den

When General Daniel Sickles marched his men forward from their original position on Cemetery Ridge, his left flank rested here with Captain James Smith's artillery battery. This was a horrible place for artillery. The jumble of rocks prevented the limbers, or ammunition chests, from being close to the guns, making it time consuming to resupply the guns.

At around 4:00 p.m. the Confederates opened their attack from Warfield Ridge and headed straight for these rocks. Confederate soldiers from Texas, Georgia and Alabama launched numerous assaults against Smith's battery and eventually overtook it. The nature of the boulders provided a safe haven for Confederate sharpshooters who spent the rest of the evening firing at Union soldiers on Little Round Top.

Following the battle, this area became very popular with photographers who came to visit the battlefield. When the photographers arrived, they were greeted to a horrific scene in the area around Little Round Top and Devil's Den. On this part of the battlefield there were still many soldiers who had not yet been buried. Turning their camera lenses toward these men, photographers like Mathew Brady, Timothy O'Sullivan and Alexander Gardner, captured, printed and displayed the horrors of war for civilians back home.

Several sections of the battlefield received new names as a result of the terrible carnage wrought there. The Slaughter Pen was the area between the Round Tops and Devil's Den and the Valley of Death followed Plum Run. Even today, more than a hundred years later, the photographs recorded here provide a haunting and grizzly reminder of the cruelty of war, and the ferocity of the fighting that occurred on the soil upon which you now stand.

Sunrise in Devil's Den

Devil's Den

This photograph, taken four and a half months after the battle, provides a revealing view of the terrain in 1863.

Devil's Den

2. This photograph by Alexander Gardner shows two dead Confederate soldiers in the area known as the Slaughter Pen

DEVIL'S DEN

Little Round Top ⑧

Devil Den ③ ② ①
8a

Plum Run

Bloody Run

The Slaughter Pen

PHOTOGRAPHY FINDER
Compare the past with the present. Use this quick guide to find the locations where famous battlefield photographs were taken.

Devil's Den

3 This photograph of a dead Confederate sharpshooter became one of the most recognized images of the Battle of Gettysburg. Later investigations revealed, however, that the photographer had moved the soldier's body to this location and staged the scene.

Devil's Den

THE WHEATFIELD

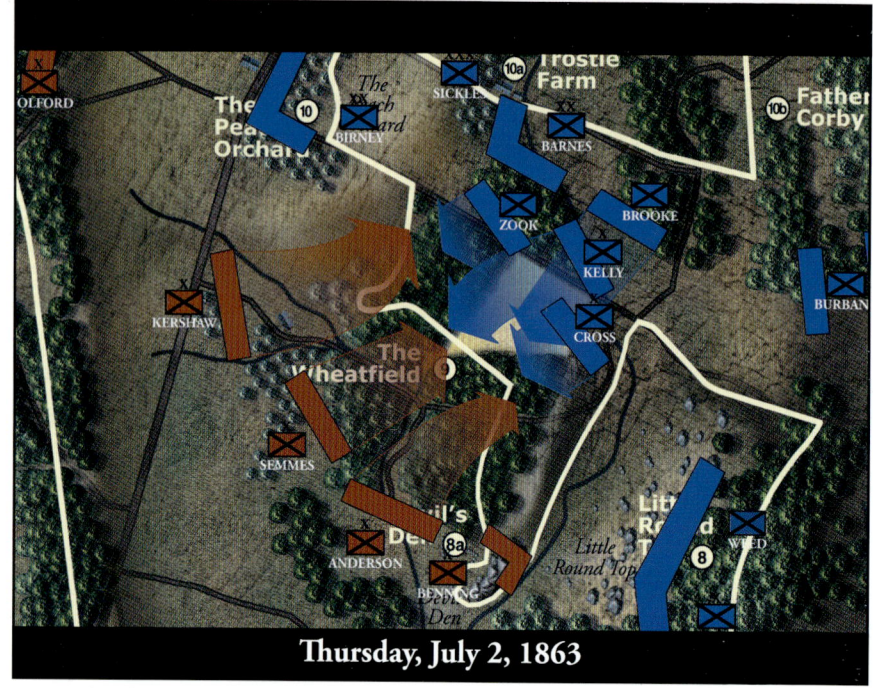

Thursday, July 2, 1863

During the afternoon of July 2, the Wheatfield witnessed some of the heaviest fighting of the entire Civil War, as the contested ground exchanged hands several times.

HARRISON JEFFORDS

Shortly before Gettysburg, the 4th Michigan infantry received a new flag to carry into battle. When the Governor of Michigan and a senator visited the regiment in camp, the unit's commander, Colonel Harrison Jeffords, made them a solemn promise: he would protect that flag with his life and it would never fall into enemy hands. On the second day at Gettysburg, in the raging battle in the Wheatfield, Jeffords spotted the flag about to be carried off by the Confederates. With a sword in his hand, he immediately rushed at the enemy. Slashing wildly, he brought down several of the Confederates, until he himself was bayoneted to death. Witnessing this sight, Jeffords' brother, serving in the same regiment, fended off the Confederates with his sword. Jeffords lost his life during the struggle but held true to his promise and saved the flag. The men of his command paid tribute to their fallen leader with a depiction of him on the regiment's battlefield monument (right).

THE WHEATFIELD

Colonel Edward Cross

Colonel Edward Cross had served for a time in the Mexican Army, and when the Civil War began he immediately returned to the United States and was commissioned colonel of the 5th New Hampshire. In time, he rose to brigade commander. Though he reportedly had survived 12 woundings during the first two years of the war, Cross soon began to doubt his ability to continue much longer. Prior to the battle, Colonel Cross stated to his staff the possibility that this battle would be his last. He even went as far as to have his staff assemble his personal belongings and prepare them to be sent back to New Hampshire.

As the brigade prepared for battle, Colonel Cross had one thing left to do. Ritualistically, before every battle, Cross had a staff officer tie a red bandana around his head. On July 2 the bandana was black. General Winfield Scott Hancock, 2nd Corps commander, rode up and addressed Cross prior to the action. *"Colonel Cross,"* he said, *"this is the last battle you will fight without a star,"* meaning that Hancock was going to promote Colonel Cross to general. Cross looked at Hancock and said *"General, you can keep your star. This will be my last battle."* With that, Cross and his brigade entered the fray where he fell mortally wounded.

PEACH ORCHARD

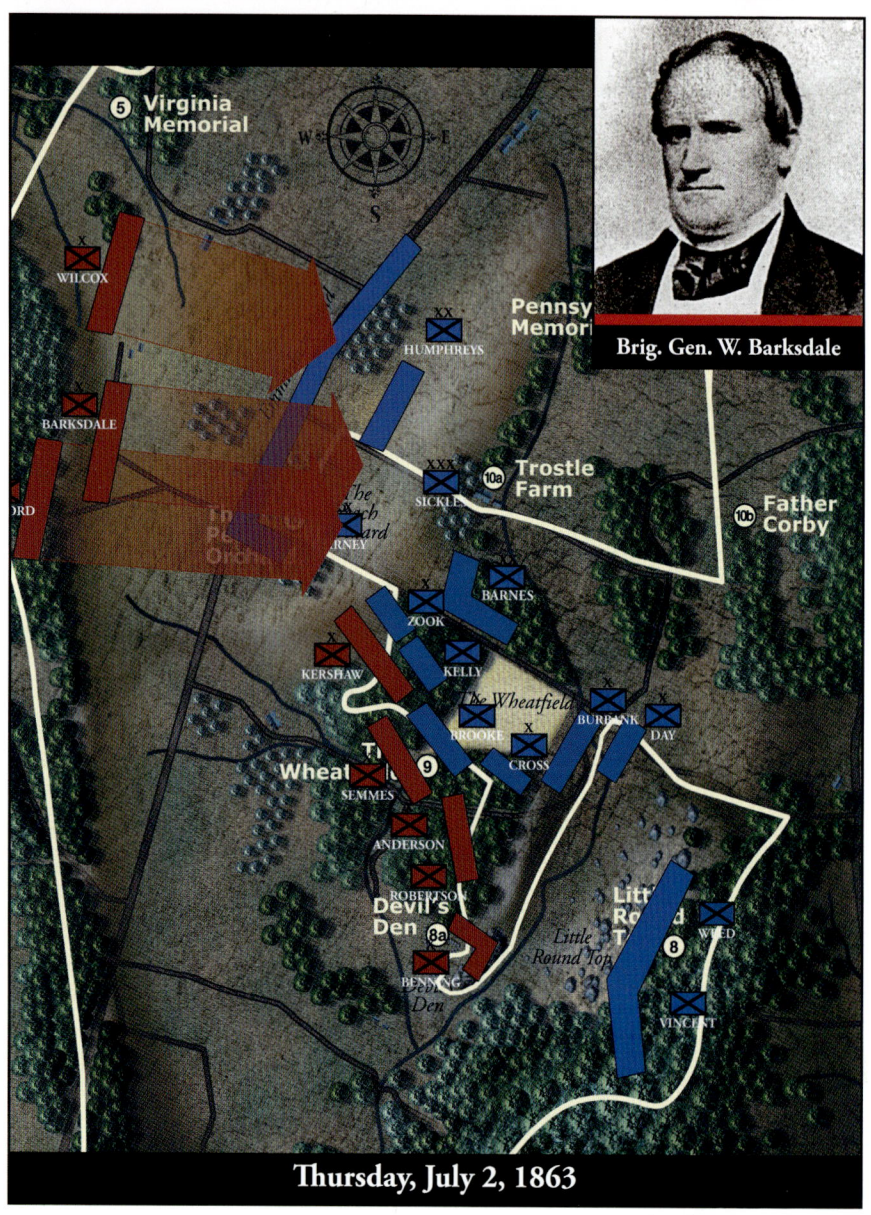

Thursday, July 2, 1863

Brig. Gen. W. Barksdale

General William Barksdale's attack on the Peach Orchard split the Union 3rd Corps in two. A soldier in the 22nd Massachusetts later recalled the chaotic scene that ensued: *"The hoarse and indistinguishable orders of commanding officers, the screaming and bursting of shells, canister and shrapnel as they tore through the struggling masses of humanity, the death screams of wounded animals, the groans of their human companions, wounded and dying and trampled underfoot by hurrying batteries, riderless horses and the moving lines of battle-a perfect Hell on earth, never, perhaps to be equaled, certainly not to be surpassed, nor ever to be forgotten in a man's lifetime. It has never been effaced from my memory, day or night, for fifty years."*

60

PEACH ORCHARD

Major General Daniel Sickles

General Daniel Sickles was a controversial figure even before the Civil War began. In 1859, he had recently been elected to the United States Congress from a New York City district. While in Washington, Sickles learned that his wife Teresa was having an affair with a brilliant young attorney, Philip Barton Key, the son of Francis Scott Key, author of the *Star Spangled Banner*. Philip Key was not only a well-known attorney in Washington D.C., he was the district attorney, the chief prosecutor of the nation's capital. When Sickles saw Key outside his home in Lafayette Park, directly across from the White House, he became enraged. *"Key, you scoundrel,"* yelled Sickles, *"you have dishonored my bed – you must die!"* In broad daylight Sickles shot Key twice and killed him.

Arrested and charged with the crime, it became the trial of the century. Sickles assembled a lawyer team that was second to none and pleaded temporary insanity. He was one of the first persons to enter that type of plea and was acquitted!

Teresa Sickles   Philip Key

The Excelsior Brigade consisted of five New York regiments that General Daniel Sickles commanded earlier in the Civil War. The men of those regiments were called in to assist their former commander when the Union 3rd Corps began to crumble under the Confederate attacks on July 2, 1863. Their monument (right) stands in a location central to where the regiments fought that day.

TROSTLE FARM

SICKLE'S LEG

As the Confederates overran the Peach Orchard, General Sickles (left) was sitting atop his horse near the Trostle barn. He was observing his troops when a Confederate artillery round struck him in the right leg, nearly tearing it off. Sickles was carried off the field and his leg amputated. Sent to Washington, D.C., Sickles recuperated from his wounds while his leg bones (below) were put on display at what is today the National Museum of Health and Medicine. Sickles himself often visited his leg for many years after the battle.

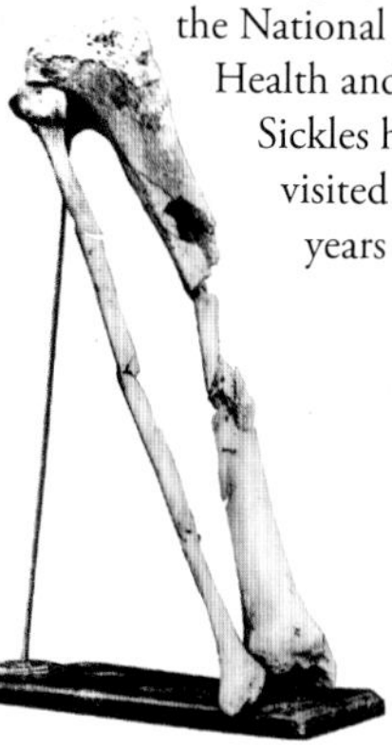

Maj. Gen. Daniel Sickles

Notice the cannonball hole still visible to this day.

TROSTLE FARM

This sketch is of the 5th MA battery attempting to tow their gun past the Trostle barn to safety, as Bigelow's battery covers their retreat.

Capt. John Bigelow

Bigelow's Defense

When Barksdale's brigade crashed through the Union line in the Peach Orchard, a chaotic Union withdrawl ensued, as a line of Federal artillery along the Wheatfield Road attempted to limber up and retreat. Captain John Bigelow's 9th MA battery was called upon to cover their exit, and sacrifice themselves if necessary. Bigelow ordered a "retreat by prolonge," a maneuver in which the guns are pulled in retreat, aided by the recoil of the gun's firing. Unfortunately the battery's retreat was too slow. Confederates rushed the cannon and hand-to-hand fighting ensued. Four guns were captured, but later recovered.

Father Corby

Father Corby

Father William Corby was a holy cross father, chaplain of the 88th NY, one of the regiments of the famed Irish Brigade. On the afternoon of July 2, when the men of this brigade were ordered into battle to bolster the faltering 3rd Corps, he asked permission of Colonel Patrick Kelly, commander of the Irish Brigade, if he could delay the men for just a moment to say some words. Kelly assented and the men removed their hats and knelt down, while the sounds of battle could be heard raging all around them. Father Corby stood atop a boulder, raised his right hand, and asked God to grant the men courage and final absolution. And with that, the men marched into battle.

Father William Corby

Father Corby

Absolution Under Fire
Image courtesy of University of Notre Dame

Pennsylvania Memorial

Colonel William Colvill

Charge of the 1st Minnesota

At about 7:00 pm on July 2, in the last remaining light of the day, General Winfield Scott Hancock rode to this area in time to spot some 1,700 Alabama soldiers heading toward the sparsely defended center of the Union line. Desperately in need of troops, Hancock spied the only regiment nearby, the 1st Minnesota Volunteer Infantry.

The 1st Minnesota had the distinction of being the very first Union regiment sworn into Federal service at the start of the American Civil War. When President Abraham Lincoln asked for 75,000 volunteers early in 1861, Governor Alexander Ramsey of Minnesota happened to be in Washington on the day of Lincoln's call-to-arms. Enthusiastically, the governor stopped the Secretary of War, Simon Cameron, on the street and pledged the first 1,000 men to the Union cause. Thus by late April, just two weeks after the bombardment of Fort Sumter, the 1st Minnesota was mustered into Federal service and on July 2nd, 1863, it numbered 262 men present for duty along Cemetery Ridge.

Riding up to the men of the 1st Minnesota, General Hancock exclaimed, *"My god, are these all the men we have here."* Then turning to Colonel William Colvill, commander of the 1st Minnesota, he shouted, *"Advance Colonel and take those colors,"* pointing to the Confederate flags advancing toward Cemetery Ridge. The 262 men of the 1st Minnesota rushed into the thicket of woods to the west of the ridge and slammed into the Alabamians. Within fifteen minutes 82 percent of the small Midwest regiment was killed, wounded, or captured, one of the highest Union regimental losses of the war.

The desperate measure had worked, however. In the smoke and confusion of the charge, the 1st Minnesota checked the forward momentum of the Confederates, giving Hancock just enough time to rush reinforcements in to breach the gap. The left end of the Union line remained intact.

PENNSYLVANIA MEMORIAL

PENNSYLVANIA MEMORIAL

The Pennsylvania State Memorial was dedicated in 1910. It cost $182,000 to complete and required 1,252 tons of cut granite to build. Architect W. Liance Cottrell's design was selected from among fifty-one designs and thirty plaster models that were submitted as part of a contest to design the monument. Cottrell received $500 for his winning design. The monument is meant to honor all the Pennsylvanians who participated in the campaign.

Standing atop the dome is the "Goddess of Peace and Victory." Sculpted by Samuel Murray, the bronze statue stands twenty-one feet tall and weighs 7,500 pounds.

Twenty-five ton granite monoliths that depict battle scenes honoring the four branches of the army (infantry, cavalry, artillery, and signal corps) are positioned above each of the archways.

Ninety bronze tablets contain the 34,500 names of every Pennsylvania soldier who was present during the Gettysburg campaign. Each tablet represents a single regiment and the soldiers' names are organized according to company. A star next to an individual's name identifies those who were killed or mortally wounded in the battle.

1st Minnesota Monument

Spangler's Spring

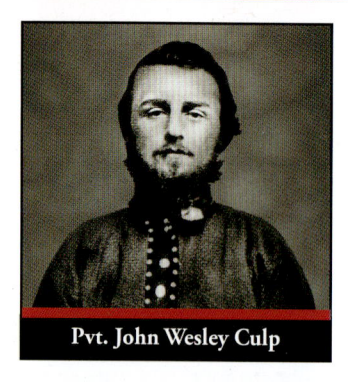

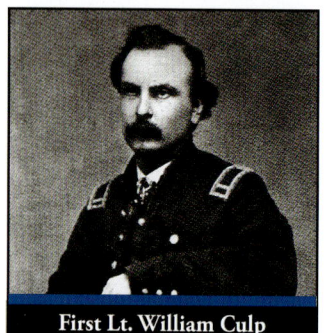

Pvt. John Wesley Culp

First Lt. William Culp

Cpl. Johnston "Jack" Skelly, Jr.

Mary Virginia "Jennie" Wade

Gettysburg Friends

One of the Confederate soldiers who participated in the fighting near Culp's Hill was a young man by the name of John Wesley Culp. A member of the famed Stonewall Brigade, Company B, 2nd Virginia Infantry Regiment, "Wes" as he was known, was no stranger to these woods. He had grown up in the area and his cousin, Henry Culp, owned a portion of this hill.

Prior to the war, Wesley had worked in the carriage industry for C.W. Hoffman in Gettysburg. But in 1856, the Hoffman's carriage business moved south to Shepherdstown, VA and Wesley followed. By the time the war broke out, Wesley's sympathies lay with the South. He enlisted in the Confederate Army, while his brother and many of his Gettysburg friends joined the Union Army.

One of Wesley's friends, Jack Skelly Jr. had enlisted in the 87th Pennsylvania Infantry, Company F along with Wesley's brother, William. In June 1863, as part of the Confederate advance into the North, Lee's army clashed with Union forces at Winchester, Virginia about ninety miles south of Gettysburg. During the battle, Jack Skelly was mortally wounded. By sheer coincidence, as Wesley's regiment was moving through Winchester on the way north, he saw Skelly dying in Confederate hands. The two men spoke and Skelly asked Wesley to relay a message to a young lady whom he was quite fond of, if Wes arrived near Gettysburg. That young woman was Mary Virginia "Jennie" Wade.

As fate would have it, Wes found himself here in Gettysburg at the beginning of July 1863, fighting on the fields where he had grown up. At some point, Wesley visited his sisters here in town and relayed the story of meeting Skelly, but was unable to personally deliver the message to Jennie. Sometime on July 2 or 3, the exact date is not known, Wesley was killed in action. He was the only member of his company to be killed in action here at the Battle of Gettysburg.

Jennie's life would also be claimed by the fighting in Gettysburg, the only civilian killed during the battle. And Jack Skelly? He succumbed to his wound on July 12, 1863. Three friends from Gettysburg — all victims of the American Civil War.

Spangler's Spring

Charge of the 2nd Massachusetts

On July 3, the Union 12th Corps sought to retake a series of earthworks near Spangler's Spring that had been occupied by Union forces the day before. The plan was to send in skirmishers to probe for enemy resistance and follow with an infantry attack, if the Confederate flank was weak. Through an error in communications, however, Colonel Charles Mudge, commander of the 2nd MA, was ordered to launch a full-scale assault. Completely dumbfounded, Mudge asked, *"Are you sure that is the order?"* After assurances were given, Mudge exclaimed, *"Well, it is murder, but it's the order."* Then, turning to his men he shouted, *"Up men; over the works. Forward. Double quick."*

The 2nd Massachusetts charged out from the cover of the woods into the open meadow. Three Confederate regiments fired into the advancing Bay State troops, littering the field with their bodies. The ill-fated charge resulted in 45 deaths, including that of Colonel Mudge.

Colonel Charles Mudge

Meadow over which the 2nd MA charged on July 3

Culp's Hill

149th New York Infantry

The fighting on Culp's Hill centered around the Union earthworks which ran along the hill from the base to the top. These shallow trenches were the key to the Union defense of the hill. From behind this protective barrier, soldiers of a lone Federal brigade, numbering only 1,300 men, were able to hold at bay nearly 6,000 Confederate soldiers attacking the hill.

The fighting was extremely heavy at times. Bullets and bursting cannon shells tore through the woods covering the hill causing extraordinary devastation. One story that illustrates the intensity of the fire on this end of the battlefield is that of the 149th New York infantry. After two days of battle on Culp's Hill the American flag of this regiment was inspected. It had eighty-one bullet holes through its red, white, and blue field. The staff, which carried the banner, had been struck by Confederate bullets seven times!

At one point during the fight the staff was shot in two by Confederate gunfire. In the heat of battle, under heavy fire, Color Sergeant William C. Lilly reached to the ground, grabbed a piece of wood from a nearby box, and with straps from his backpack, spliced the flag staff back together. A courageous act, and one that is forever immortalized on the bronze relief that adorns the 149th NY monument here on Culp's Hill.

CULP'S HILL

This photograph, taken after the battle, shows an example of the Federal breastworks on Culp's Hill that played a crucial role in the Union defense.

CULP'S HILL

Brigadier General George Greene

At age 62, Brigadier General Greene was the oldest Union general on the battlefield. He graduated second in his class at West Point in 1823 and was an engineer by training. On the morning of July 2, Greene suggested that men of the Union 12th Corps construct earthworks all along the defensive perimeter of the hill. The breastworks were not elaborate, but they proved invaluable to the Union defenders.

On the evening of July 2, after the 12th Corps vacated this area to support the Union left, Confederate General Richard Ewell assaulted Culp's Hill with three full brigades. Left to defend the extreme right end of the Union line were five New York regiments, under the command of General Greene.

Outnumbered by more than three to one, Greene's New Yorkers inflicted more than six times the number of casualties on their enemy and ultimately maintained control of the summit. Upon Greene's death in 1899, his former soldiers paid tribute to him by placing a 4,000 pound boulder from Culp's Hill over his grave in Warwick, Rhode Island.

Culp's Hill

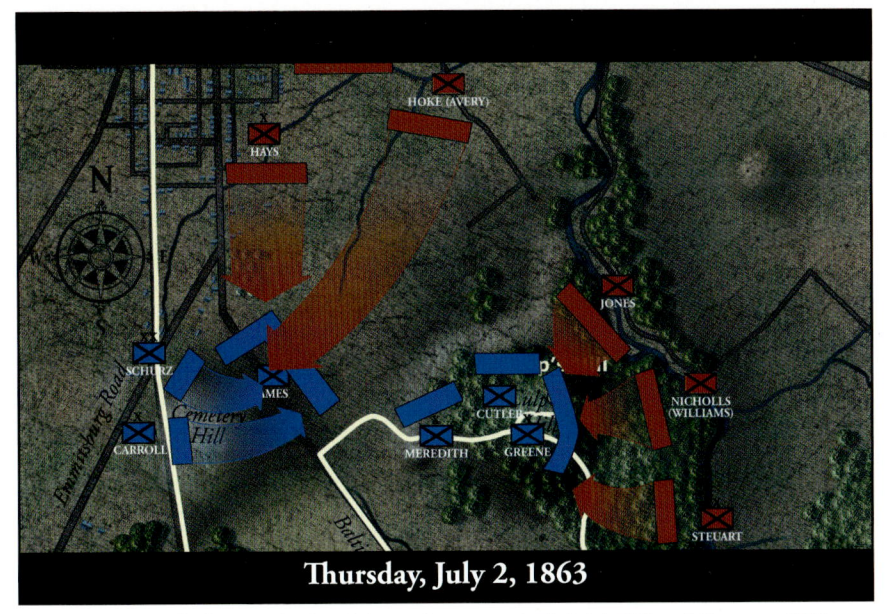

Thursday, July 2, 1863

On the evening of July 2, 1863, Confederate forces attacked Culp's Hill and Cemetery Hill. While unable to take the summit of Culp's Hill, the Rebels did capture Cemetery Hill before being driven back.

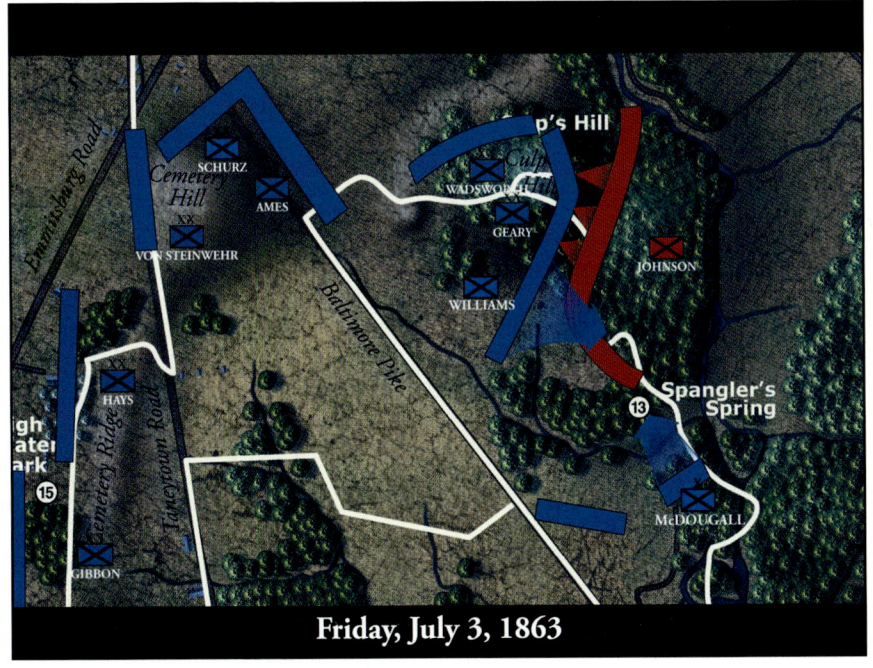

Friday, July 3, 1863

The Federals renewed the fighting on Culp's Hill early on the morning of July 3, 1863. After nearly seven hours of heavy fighting, Union forces recaptured the ground they had lost the night before at the base of Culp's Hill.

High Water Mark

High Water Mark

Pickett's Charge is often referred to as the "High Water Mark" of the Confederacy. It marks the apex of southern military achievement during the war. Never again would Lee have the men and resources to strike a decisive blow against his enemy on Northern soil. The losses suffered here at Pickett's Charge, and at Gettysburg overall, would condemn Lee and the Confederacy to a defensive struggle for the rest of the war.

On July 3, 1863, Lee announced his bold plan with one of the largest cannonades of the Civil War. At around 1:00 p.m., approximately 150 Southern cannons simultaneously began to blast the center of the Union line.

Unfortunately for Lee, the smoke from the cannons made it impossible to see where the shells were landing. After several exchanges of cannon fire with the Union Army, Lee's gunners could not see that their shells were drifting back behind the main Union line of battle, leaving the troops in front relatively intact and prepared to meet the assault.

Shortly after 3:00 p.m. approximately 6,000 Union soldiers positioned along Cemetery Ridge strained their eyes due west across the open fields and saw a long gray line, nearly a mile in length. No one could help but to admire the courage of these men lined up in perfect rows.

Then the great bloodletting began. Union gun crews had ceased firing prior to the Confederate assault in an effort to conserve ammunition. When the Confederates marched forward, the Union gun crews took careful aim and began firing shot and shell into their ranks with deadly impact. One Union gunner later recalled how a single shell felled ten men. Huge holes were blown in the Confederate lines, yet they still closed ranks and pressed forward. The momentum was too much for cannons alone to stop. Soon, the entire

HIGH WATER MARK

Artist, Frederick Rothermel's depiction of Pickett's Charge

middle of the Union line was literally ablaze with infantry fire. When the Confederates reached the Emmitsburg Road, thousands of Union muskets discharged nearly at the same moment, unleashing a devastating volley into the front lines of Pickett's men. For the next several minutes, the Confederates withstood fire from 6,000 Union troops and close range canister fire. Many survivors of the charge likened it to walking through a hailstorm. The fire was so heavy that one of the fence planks along the Emmitsburg Road counted 836 holes when inspected after the battle.

And yet despite the carnage and the loss of men, the Confederates still surged forward. Eventually they reached the small stone wall, an area that became known as "The Angle." After crossing almost a mile of open ground this stone wall was the first element of protection some of the Confederates could take advantage of. Yet, to break the Union line, they would have to press forward.

General Lewis Armistead placed his hat upon his sword and rallied the men, *"Give them the cold steel boys."* With that, he and his men surged over the wall and charged the Union troops. This final desperate surge was not enough. Union soldiers crowded in on all sides firing at point blank range. In the melee, General Armistead was mortally wounded, shot in the arm and leg. The approximate location where he fell is today marked by the small scroll granite monument in the middle of The Angle.

Soon after Armistead was wounded, the Confederate assault lost its momentum and began to disintegrate. Most of those who stepped over the wall with him were either killed or captured. Those who could, tried to make their way back across the field of death, once again having to brave the musket and cannon fire on their path of retreat.

HIGH WATER MARK

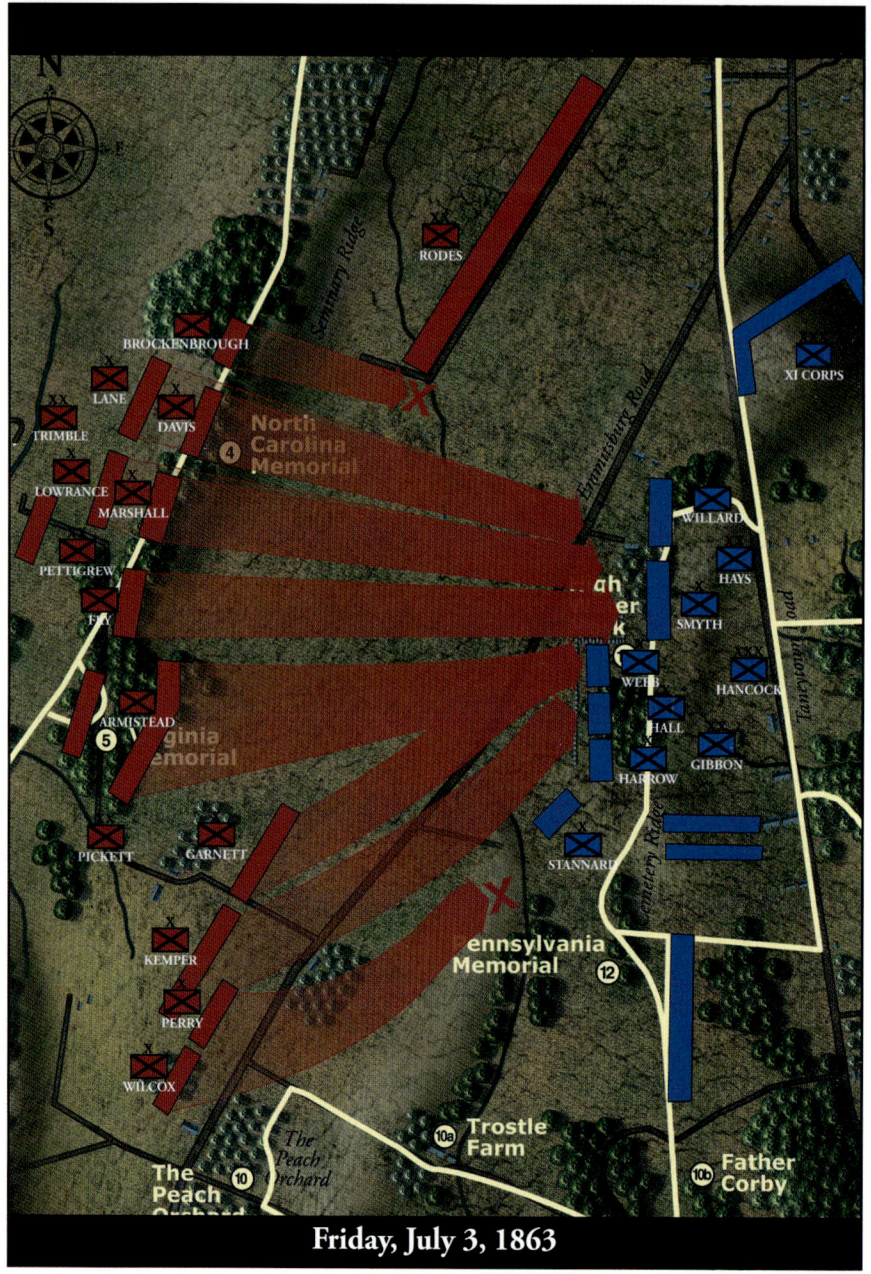

Friday, July 3, 1863

For two full hours Confederate gun crews bombarded the Union defenses along Cemetery Ridge. Then at around 3:00 p.m. in the afternoon, some 12,500 Confederate troops emerged from along Seminary Ridge and began their assault on the center of the Union line.

High Water Mark

Major General George Pickett

George Pickett was born in Richmond, VA in 1825, the son of a prominent Old Virginia family and cousin of future Confederate general, Henry Heth. At the age of 17 he received an appointment to the United States Military Academy. His lackluster performance at West Point, however, earned Pickett the nickname "goat," a moniker bestowed on the student who graduates at the bottom of the class. Upon graduation, he was assigned to the infantry and soon saw action in the Mexican War. At the Battle of Chapultepec, he distinguished himself when he grabbed the American flag from the hands of a wounded James Longstreet (his eventual commander at Gettysburg), and stormed the enemy's parapet, tore down the Mexican flag, and raised the Stars and Stripes. When the Civil War began he resigned his commission in order to fight for the South. At Gettysburg, Pickett's men spent the first two days of the battle near Chambersburg guarding wagon trains and destroying railroad tracks, unaware of the infamy that would befall them on July 3.

HIGH WATER MARK

Brig. General Lewis Armistead

Maj. Gen. Winfield Scott Hancock

A Tale of Two Friends

Prior to the Civil War, Confederate General Lewis Armistead was a close friend of Union General Winfield Scott Hancock. Both men were officers in the regular army, stationed in California. In May 1861, Mrs. Almira Hancock held a farewell gathering for the Southern officers who had resigned their commissions in order to join the Confederate cause. That was the last happy time the two men would share. Before departing, Armistead gave Mrs. Hancock his prayer book. Almost two years later, Armistead would end up leading a major portion of Pickett's assault against Hancock's position on July 3, 1863.

High Water Mark

Haunted Memories

Survivors of Pickett's Charge would never be able to forget the terror of that day. One of the most moving accounts of a soldier's experience comes from Capt. Henry T. Owen of the 18th Virginia volunteers. Owen would survive Pickett's Charge and the American Civil War. Almost six months after Pickett's Charge, he was still deeply disturbed by a dream that plagued him. Describing the dream to his wife in a letter, he wrote that in the dream he would find himself once again on the fields of Gettysburg, marching into battle with his old friends. But this time there was a thin shadow in front of him. Although nearly transparent, he could not get around it. No matter what he did it would always stay between him and the enemy. When the fighting was done and he was out of harms reach, the shadow would speak to him and it would say, *I am the angel that protected you. I will never leave nor forsake you.* The surprise was so great that he awoke and burst into tears. His first thought being, what had he done that should entitle him to such favor beyond the hundreds of brave and reputed good men who had fallen on that day, leaving behind mothers, wives, orphaned children, and disconsolate families to mourn their fates.

Capt. Henry Owen

In the picture below, surviving members of Pickett's Charge reenacted the historic event during the grand reunion of 1913.

Bibliography

Association of Licensed Battlefield Guides. "Cemetery Hill: Witness to History" A Seminar Map Booklet, April 2000.

Bachelder, John B. *Bachelder's Gettysburg Battlefield Maps.* 27 maps. Dayton, OH: Morningside Books, nd.

Boatner, Mark Mayo, III. *The Civil War Dictionary.* New York, NY: David McKay Company, Inc., 1959.

Brandy, Ken and Florance Freeland comps. *The Gettysburg Papers.* Volumes 1 and 2. Dayton, OH: Morningside Books, 1986.

Busey, John W., and David G. Martin. *Regimental Strengths and Losses at Gettysburg.* Hightstown, NJ: Longstreet House, 1994.

Clark, Champ ed. *Gettysburg The Confederate High Tide.* Time-Life Series The Civil War. Alexandria, VA: Time-Life Books, Inc, 1985.

Coco, Gregory A. *A Vast Sea of Misery.* Gettysburg, PA: Thomas Publications, 1988.

_____. *On The Bloodstain Field.* Gettysburg, PA: Thomas Publications, 1987.

_____. *On The Bloodstain Field II.* Gettysburg, PA: Thomas Publications, 1989.

Coddington, Edwin B. *The Gettysburg Campaign A Study in Command.* New York, NY: Charles Scribner's Sons, 1968.

Coffin, Howard. *Nine Months to Gettysburg Standard's Vermonters and the Repulse of Pickett's Charge.* Woodstock, VT: The Countryman Press, 1997.

Cole, James M., and Roy E. Frampton. *Lincoln and the Human Interest Stories of the Gettysburg National Cemetery.* Gettysburg, PA, 1995.

Desjardin, Thomas A. *Stand Firm Ye Boys of Maine: The 20th Maine and the Gettysburg Campaign.* Gettysburg, PA: Thomas Publications, 1995.

Frassanito, William A. *Early Photography at Gettysburg.* Gettysburg, PA: Thomas Publications, 1995.

Freeman, Douglas Southall. *R. E. Lee A Biography.* 4 Volumes. New York, NY: Charles Scribner's Sons, 1934-1935.

Gettysburg Magazine Articles of Lasting Interest. Issues 1-22. Dayton, OH: Morningside Books, 1989-2000.

Gordon, John B. *Reminiscenes of the Civil War.* New York, NY: Charles Schribner's Sons, 1904.

Grant, Ulysses S. *Memoirs and Selected Letters.* New York, NY: Literary Classics of the United States, Inc., 1990.

Harrison, Kathy George. *Nothing But Glory Pickett's Division at Gettysburg.* Gettysburg, PA: Thomas Publications, 1993.

Hassler, Warren W., Jr. *Crisis at the Crossroads the First Day at Gettysburg.* Montgomery, AL: University of Alabama Press, 1970.

Hawthorne, Frederick W. *Gettysburg: Stories of Men and Monuments as Told by the Battlefield Guides.* Gettysburg, PA: Association of Licensed Battlefield Guides, 1988.

Imhof, John D. *Gettysburg: Day Two A Study in Maps.* Baltimore, MD: Butternut and Blue, 1999.

Maine at Gettysburg Commission. *Maine at Gettysburg: Report of the Maine Commissioners.* Portland, ME: Lakeside Press, 1898.

Martin, David. *Gettysburg, July 1.* Conshohocken, PA: Combined Books, 1995.

Motts, Wayne E. *"Trust In God and Fear Nothing" General Lewis A. Armistead, CSA.* Gettysburg, PA: Farnsworth House Military Impressions, 1994.

New York Monuments Commission. *Final Report of the Battlefield of Gettysburg.* 3 Volumes Albany, NY: J.B. Lyon Company, 1900

Nolan, Alan T. *The Iron Brigade a Military History.* Berrien Springs, MI: Hardscrabble Books, 1983.

Peters, James Edward. *Arlington National Cemetery: Shrine to American Heroes.* Kensington, MD: Woodbine House, 1986.

Pfanz, Harry W. *Gettysburg the Second Day.* Chapel Hill, NC: University of North Carolina Press, 1987.

_____. *Gettysburg Culp's Hill and Cemetery Hill.* Chapel Hill, NC: University of North Carolina Press, 1993.

Phipps, Michael A. *"The Devil's To Pay" General John Buford, USA.* Gettysburg, PA: Farnsworth House Military Impressions, 1995.

Raus, Edmund J., Jr. *A Generation on the March: The Union Army at Gettysburg.* Gettysburg, PA: Thomas Publications, 1996.

Reardon, Carol. *Pickett's Charge in History and Memory.* Chapel Hill, NC: University of North Carolina Press, 1997.

Reese, Timothy. *Sykes' Regular Infantry Division, 1861-1864. A History of Regular United States Infantry Operations in the Civil War's Eastern Theater.* Jefferson, NC: McFarland & Co., 1990.

Riley, Michael. *"For God's Sake Forward!" General John F. Reynolds, USA.* Gettysburg, PA: Farnsworth House Military Impressions, 1995.

Shue, Richard S. *Morning At Willoughby Run July 1, 1863.* Gettysburg, PA: Thomas Publications, 1995.

Small, Cindy L. *The Jennie Wade Story.* Gettysburg, PA: Thomas Publications, 1991.

Smith, Timothy H. and Garry E. Adelman. *Devil's Den A History and Guide.* Gettysburg, PA: Thomas Publications, 1997.

Stevens, C. A. *Berdan's United States Sharpshooters in the Army of the Potomac.* reprint, Dayton, OH: Morningside Books, 1984.

Stewart, George R. *Pickett's Charge A Microhistory of the Final Attack at Gettysburg, July 3, 1863.* reprint, Dayton, OH: Morningside Books, 1983.

Swanburg, W. A. *Sickles the Incredible.* New York, NY: Charles Scribner's Sons, 1956.

War Department. *The Official Records of the War of the Rebellion: A Compilation of the Official Records of the Union and Confederate Armies.* Series I. Volume 27. Parts 1-3. Washington, DC: GPO, 1889.

Wiley, Bell I. *The Life of Billy Yank The Common Soldier of the Union.* Reprint, New York, NY: Doubleday & Company, Inc., 1971.

_____. *The Life of Johnny Reb The Common Soldier of the Confederacy.* New York, NY: Doubleday & Company, Inc., 1971.

Editor
Angela Atkinson

Voice Credits
Introduction: Reg Green, Driving Guide: Phyllis Hamlin, Historian Narrator: Wayne Motts

Photography Credits
Warren Motts and the Motts Military Museum, Adams County Historical Society, United States Military History Institute, Gettysburg National Military Park, Richard Kohr, Leib Archives, Library of Congress, Maine State Archives, North Carolina Department of Cultural Resources, National Museum of Health and Medicine, University of Notre Dame, Minnesota State Archive, Michigan State Archive, Dirty Billy's Hats, www.dirtybillyshats.com, Gallon Historical Art, Gettysburg, PA, www.gallon.com.

Designed and developed in the USA. Printed in India.

THE NATIONAL CIVIL WAR MUSEUM

IN ASSOCIATION WITH THE SMITHSONIAN INSTITUTION

Visit our Museum after touring the battlefield

Show this ad and save up to $6.00 off!
($1 per person off of our general admission for up to 6 people)
Cannot be combined with any other discounts.

OPEN 7 DAYS A WEEK
Except New Years Day, Easter, Thanksgiving & Christmas

1 Lincoln Circle at Reservoir Park
Harrisburg, PA
866.BLU.GRAY
www.NationalCivilWarMuseum.org

Travel adventures that leave you smarter!

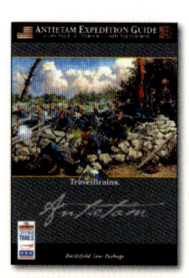

ANTIETAM

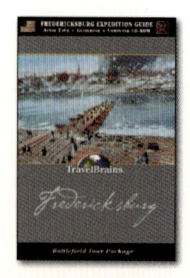

FREDERICKSBURG

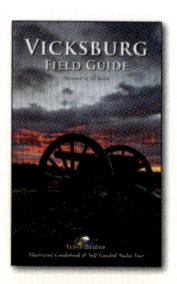

VICKSBURG

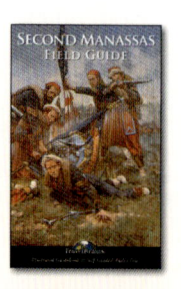

2ND MANASSAS

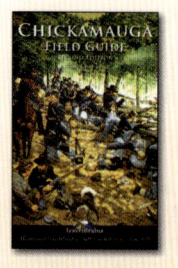

CHICKAMAUGA

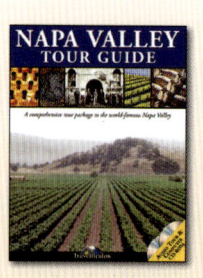

NAPA VALLEY

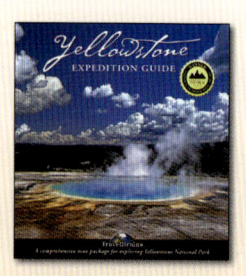

YELLOWSTONE

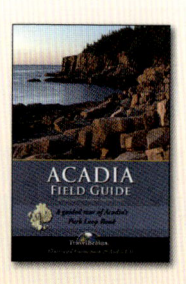

ACADIA

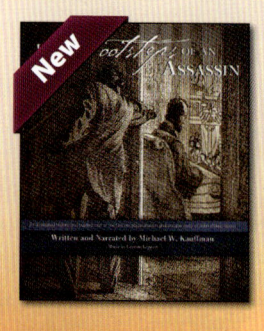

IN THE FOOTSTEPS OF AN ASSASSIN

164-page illustrated history of the plot to assassinate Lincoln and a guided tour of the escape route of John Wilkes Booth. Written and narrated by the country's leading expert on the Lincoln assassination, Michael W. Kauffman.

TravelBrains®
Travel adventures that leave you smarter!

Visit TravelBrains.com to see our entire selection of self-guided tours

Yellowstone Expedition Guide

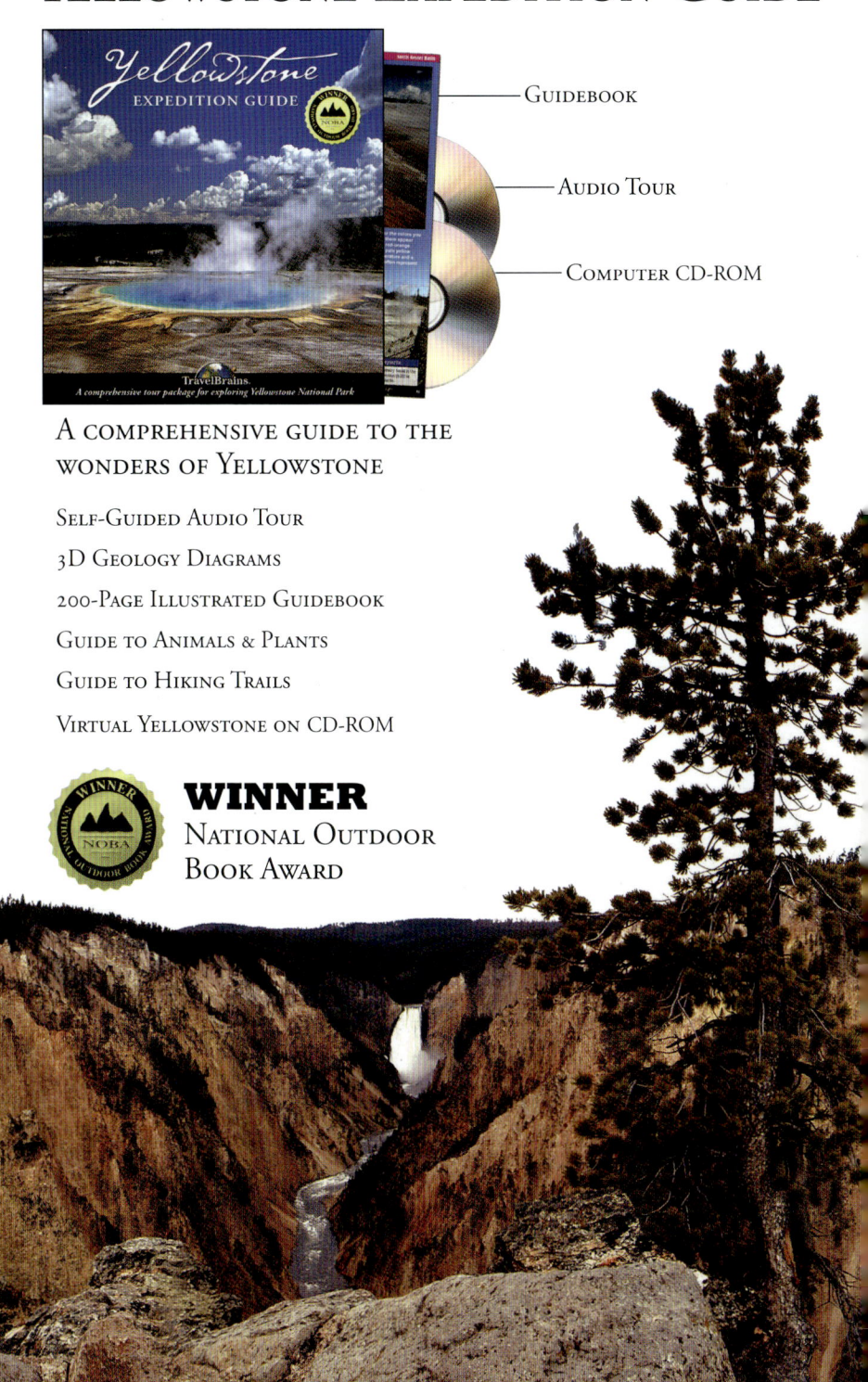

- Guidebook
- Audio Tour
- Computer CD-ROM

A comprehensive guide to the wonders of Yellowstone

Self-Guided Audio Tour

3D Geology Diagrams

200-Page Illustrated Guidebook

Guide to Animals & Plants

Guide to Hiking Trails

Virtual Yellowstone on CD-ROM

WINNER
National Outdoor Book Award